For Swi 365 MAIN SETS

By – Andrew Starykowicz

I would like to thank Kristan for motivating me to put this together.

I would also like to thank my coaches:
Jackie, Schuable, Mike, Doug, Chris, Bob, and Karl
for pushing my limits in the pool.

StarZone LLC

For Swimmers 365 MAIN SETS

This book was inspired by swimmers I have met over the years who train in small groups or on their own repeating the same boring sets over and over. When I set out to write this book I was surprised at the limited workout material that was available for swimmers. The goal was to take my favorite workouts and share them with you to increase your workout creativity which will transfer into positive results.

The search for effective training sessions sent me digging through files from decades of swimming, water polo, and triathlon training. All of these workouts were compiled and over 365 great workouts emerged as a large mess. By eliminating the warm ups and cool downs the workouts cut down to a manageable list of main sets. The sets were then divided up by length in time and type of workout. Take these workouts and tweak them to suit your needs as an athlete and strive for your dreams. Swim hard and swim fast.

Swimming is a strenuous physical exercise that can be a dangerous activity. There are inherent risks in any physical activity; swimming is no exception. For Swimmers 365 Main Sets has published 365 sets to inspire variations of training. These workouts are guidelines and each athlete must adjust these sets based on ability level in order to safely train within the boundaries of their own capabilities. Duplication or reproduction of these sets is strictly prohibited and prosecutable by law.

Owner's Manual:

Here is a very quick review of how to use this book. Each set has four ability levels identified as gold, silver, bronze, and novice. The sets are designed to take the same amount of time and have the same training effect regardless of ability level. Gold level workouts represent training of an elite level swim club, while bronze and novice cover interval times that are achievable for aspiring swimmers. To figure out which level best suites your ability, scan the sets and select the level is closest to your current training.

Level	Standard Send-off	Fast 100 Free	Strong 400 Free	Strong 100 IM
Gold	1:20	sub1:01	sub 4:30	sub1:10
Silver	1:30	1:07	5:00	1:20
Bronze	1:45	1:22	6:00	1:30
Novice	2:00	1:32	6:45	1:45

"Standard Send-off" refers to the interval you would start on if you were to cruise a set of 10x100's and get 10-15 seconds rest. "Fast 100 Free" refers to the time it would take to complete 100 freestyle at the end of a long workout. "Strong" 100 IM and 400 Free are the times that would be achieved during an ordinary hard workout. Both strong and fast are in reference to intensity levels and a graphic illustration of the intensity scale is below.

Exertion	Maximal	99%	95%	85%	75%	70%	66%	50%	Effortless
RPE	10	9.5	9	8.5	8	7	6	5	3
Effort	Timed All Out	Sprint Blast	Fast	Strong	Cruise	Mod	Steady	Easy	Recovery

If your level falls outside of novice, just multiply the interval time of gold level by 2 or cut the interval distance in half. If the gold level does not satisfy your speed, drop 5 seconds/100 off of the intervals.

How to read the sets:
The sets are first grouped by length based on time, (under 15 minutes, 20-25 minutes, etc.), then sorted by type of training. There are nine types of training identified in this book, which is explained below.

Test Set
- Benchmark workouts that will test the limits of any athlete

Distance
- Workouts designed to increase fitness and speed for long distance swim events or open water swims

General Fitness
- Sets that contain a mixture of strokes and intensity. These are great for building early season fitness.

Middle Distance
- Training designed for events that work the aerobic and anaerobic systems

Speed
- Sprints and fast efforts to explode away from your competition

Short Rest Intervals
- Moderate to high intensity workouts with very short rest between repeats

Stroke
- Focused training on strokes other than freestyle and IM

The book starts with two pages of test sets and is followed by more than fifty pages of early morning sets sorted by time and type.

At the top and bottom of each page, there is a time classification for how long the sets on that page will take. Then down the left column the set type is identified. Across the page reads gold, silver, bronze, and novice swim levels (which were discussed on page 5) with the set details between levels silver and bronze. This can be seen at the top of each page. Within each ability level there are 3 columns. The first column is the set distance, the center column is the number of repeats and the third column is the interval time or distance. Depending on the ability level the distance will range, but all four workouts are designed to finish at nearly the same time. In the center of the page are the details of the "Set" which contains the distance or interval followed by the task for each of the repeats. There may be notes for the different levels. Below is an example of an actual set in the book.

	Set Dist	Reps	Int			Set Dist	Reps	Int	
	Gold	Silver	SET	Bronze	Novice
Speed — 1850	9 0:45 4 2:25 6 0:45 10 0:35 3 0:45	1700 — 9 0:50 4 2:40 6 0:50 4 0:40 3 0:50	50 2:Strong/1:Fast 175 Cruise 50 2:Strong/1:Fast 25 o:Kick e:Not Free 50 2:Strong/1:Fast	1400 — 9 1:00 2 3:15 6 1:00 6 0:45 3 1:00	1300 — 9 1:05 2 3:40 6 1:05 2 0:50 3 1:05

This is a set that is listed on page 48. At the top of the page it is noted that the set is 25 to 30 minutes in length. In the left column it is noted that the set is a "Speed" set. Below is an example of how a silver and novice level swimmer would commonly see this set written:

Silver Level Swimmer's Set
9 x 50   0:50   3x {2:Strong 1:Fast}
4 x 175   2:40   Cruise
6 x 50   0:50   2x {2:Strong 1:Fast}
4 x 25   0:40   odds: Kick evens: Not Free
3 x 50   0:50   2:Strong 1:Fast

This set is a calculated mix of high tempo or "Strong" efforts and sprint or "Fast" efforts. A silver level swimmer should be doing these strong efforts consistently between 35-38 seconds and the fast efforts should be close to flat out. There are two very different types of recovery between the 50's that make up this set. The first recovery set is four longer active recovery swims. The second recovery set mixes up the energy system and gives the freestyle muscles a break isolating the legs and mixing up the strokes. Below is how the set would look for the Novice swimmer:

Novice Level Swimmer's Set

9 x 50	1:05	3x {2:Strong 1:Fast}
2 x 175	3:40	Cruise
6 x 50	1:05	2x {2:Strong 1:Fast}
2 x 25	0:50	odds: Kick evens: Not Free
3 x 50	1:05	2:Strong 1:Fast

The novice level swimmer still has a total of 18 x 50's that are at a strong and fast. The difference is instead of 4 x 175 like the silver level swimmer, there is only 2 x 175 cruise. Then later in the set the novice swimmer only has 2 x 25's with more rest before the final set of 50's. The purpose of the set is exactly the same and will take the same amount of time.

Enjoy your swimming knowing that the rest of this year you will never have to see the same set again!

There is a glossary listed on the last two pages to define or clarify any of the terms or abbreviations used throughout this book.

Time (min)	Gold Set Dist	Gold Repeats	Gold Interval	Silver Set Dist	Silver Repeats	Silver Interval	SET	Bronze Set Dist	Bronze Repeats	Bronze Interval	Novice Set Dist	Novice Repeats	Novice Interval
18	1400	7	0:40	1250	6	0:45	50 Loosen/EZ	1100	5	0:55	900	4	1:05
		R	0:10		R	0:25	Rest		R	0:15		R	0:30
		1	10:00		1	10:00	T10 - How far can you go in 10 min		1	10:00		1	10:00
		R	0:20		R	0:10	Rest		R	0:30		R	0:20
		6	0:30		6	0:35	25 Mix Strokes (no free)		4	0:45		4	0:50
25		XX	1:25		XX	1:35	100's TIL YOU BLOW / drop 1 or 2 sec off interval (#1-1:25, #2-1:24, #3-1:23.... / Go until you miss 2 in a row		XX	1:50		XX	2:00
28	1600	16	1:45	1500	15	1:55	100's odds ALL OUT; evens descending stroke count by 25 / after 4,8,12,&16---10 Sit ups&10 Pushups	1200	12	2:20	1000	10	2:35
30		6	1:05		6	1:10	75 Loosen		4	1:25		4	1:40
		XX	1:30		XX	1:35	100's sub1:01's (1:07, 1:21, 1:31) until miss 2 in a row		XX	1:45		XX	2:00
		1	2:00		1	2:15	100 EZ BK		1	2:40		1	3:00
		1	10:00		1	11:00	800 TIMED (Keep your focus)		1	12:00		1	13:30
30		4	1:30		4	1:40	100 Loosen		3	2:00		3	2:15
		XX	1:10		XX	1:15	75's 45 (49, 1:00, 1:07) or faster until miss 2 in a row		XX	1:20		XX	1:30
		1	2:00		1	2:15	100-125 EZ		1	2:40		1	3:00
		1	7:30		1	8:10	600 TIMED (be steady)		1	9:00		1	10:00
30		10	0:45		9	0:50	50 Loosen		7	1:00		6	1:10
		XX	0:25		XX	0:25	25's sub 14 (15, 18, 21) until 2 miss in a row		XX	0:30		XX	0:30
		3	2:00		3	2:15	100-125 EZ		3	2:40		3	3:00
		1	3:15		1	3:30	200 TIMED		1	4:00		1	4:25
30		8	1:05		6	1:10	75 Loosen		6	1:25		4	1:40
		XX	0:50		XX	0:50	50's sub29's (32, 39, 43) until miss 2 in a row		XX	0:55		XX	1:00
		1	2:00		1	2:15	100 EZ BK		1	2:40		1	3:00
		1	5:00		1	5:30	400 TIMED		1	6:00		1	6:45
35	2200	10	2:40	2150	10	2:55	175 o:TIMED e:Perfect Technique	1750	8	3:35	1500	6	4:05
		6	0:35		4	0:40	25 o: Bk e:Choice		2	0:50		4	0:55
		1	3:45		1	4:00	300 TIMED		1	4:30		1	5:15

9

Time (min)	Gold Set Dist	Gold Repeats	Gold Interval	Silver Set Dist	Silver Repeats	Silver Interval	SET	Bronze Set Dist	Bronze Repeats	Bronze Interval	Novice Set Dist	Novice Repeats	Novice Interval
32	2200	1	2:30	2050	1	2:40	200 Timed	1600	1	3:20	1400	1	3:45
		4	1:30		4	1:35	75 Kick Descend		4	2:00		4	2:15
		1	2:30		1	2:40	200 Timed		1	3:20		1	3:45
		4	1:45		4	1:55	125 Pull Build		4	2:20		4	2:40
		1	2:30		1	2:40	200 Timed		2	3:20		1	3:45
		4	2:15		3	2:30	150 50Free/100IM		-	-		-	-
		1	2:30		1	2:40	200 Timed		-	-		-	-
35	2200	30	0:50	2000	26	0:55	50 o:TIMED e:Perfect Technique	1750	22	1:05	1550	18	1:15
		2	1:45		2	1:55	100 IM (B&N=75 bk, br, fr)		2	1:45		2	2:00
		1	6:15		1	6:50	500 TIMED		1	7:30		1	8:30
35	2200	16	1:35	2000	14	1:45	100 o:TIMED e:Perfect Technique	1750	12	2:05	1550	10	2:25
		4	0:55		4	1:00	50 Choice		3	1:15		3	1:25
		1	5:00		1	5:30	400 TIMED		1	6:00		1	6:45
35	2200	20	1:15	2050	18	1:20	75 o:TIMED e: Perfect Technique	1850	16	1:35	1550	12	1:50
		2	1:45		2	1:55	100 50 Free/50 Not Free (B&N=75)		2	1:45		2	2:00
		1	6:15		1	5:30	500 TIMED		1	7:30		1	8:30
35	2250	14	1:55	2100	12	2:10	125 o:TIMED e:Perfect Technique	1800	10	2:35	1550	8	3:00
		4	0:55		4	1:00	50 1:Fly/Bk 2:Bk/Br 3:Br/Fr 4: Fr/Fly x25's		3	1:15		3	1:25
		1	3:45		1	4:00	300 TIMED		1	4:30		1	5:15
49	1950	12	0:30	1900	12	0:30	25 o:Drill e:Build	1750	8	0:45	1700	8	0:45
		4	9:00		4	9:00	200 From A Dive - TIMED, 100-200 EZ between		4	9:00		4	9:00
		9	0:45		8	0:50	50 Steady		7	1:00		6	1:05
49	2050	7	0:50	1950	7	0:50	50 odds - Free, evens - IM order	1850	5	1:10	1750	5	1:10
		6	6:00		6	6:00	100 From A Dive - TIMED , 100-200 EZ between		6	6:00		6	6:00
		5	1:25		4	1:35	100 Steady		4	1:50		3	2:10
49	2250	10	0:50	2100	10	0:50	50 o:Drill/Build e:IM order	1750	7	1:10	1600	7	1:10
		10	3:00		10	3:00	50 From A Dive - TIMED , 50-100 EZ between		10	3:00		10	3:00
		5	2:05		4	2:20	150 Steady		4	2:45		3	3:05

Set Type	SET	Gold Dist	Gold Repeats	Gold Interval	Silver Dist	Silver Repeats	Silver Interval	Bronze Dist	Bronze Repeats	Bronze Interval	Novice Dist	Novice Repeats	Novice Interval
General	300 Build	700	1	3:50	650	1	4:00	550	1	5:05	450	1	5:45
	50 odds:Kick-Swim x25, evens: Build		8	0:45		7	0:50		5	1:00		3	1:10
	25 Not Free	750	4	0:25	700	2	0:30	600	2	0:35	500	2	0:40
	50 Drill/Swim		4	0:45		4	0:50		2	1:00		3	1:10
	150 #1:Pull #2:K Drills #3:Strong (N=100's)		3	2:15		3	2:30		3	3:00		3	2:15
	100 Kick steady	800	2	2:00	750	2	2:10	700	1	2:40	650	1	3:00
	200 Kick Fast (B&N = 150)		1	3:00		1	3:15		1	3:00		1	3:20
	50 Kick steady		4	1:00		3	1:05		4	1:20		3	1:30
	200 Kick Fast (B&N = 150)		1	3:00		1	3:15		1	3:00		1	3:20
	3:30 Build	950	1	250	850	1	250	700	1	200	600	1	150
	1:40 Cruise		2	125		2	100		2	100		2	75
	1:55 Blast		2	125		2	100		2	100		2	100
	1:00 Not Free		4	50		4	50		4	25		4	25
	250 Cruise	1200	3	3:05	1100	3	3:25	900	2	4:10	800	2	4:40
	100 Cruise		3	1:15		2	1:25		2	1:40		2	1:55
	50 All Cruise		3	0:40		2	0:45		4	0:50		2	1:00
	100 Cruise	1200	5	1:20	1100	5	1:25	900	4	1:45	800	4	2:00
	50 Not Free		4	0:50		4	0:55		4	1:05		2	1:15
	100 FAST		5	1:10		4	1:15		3	1:30		3	1:45
Middle Distance	100 Strong	750	5	1:15	700	5	1:25	600	4	1:40	550	4	1:55
	50 free/bk		5	0:50		4	0:55		4	1:05		3	1:15
	200 Fast	1000	1	2:45	900	1	3:05	800	1	3:30	700	1	4:10
	150 Hold same pace		2	2:05		2	2:20		2	2:40		2	3:10
	100 Hold same pace		3	1:25		3	1:35		2	1:50		1	2:10
	50 Hold same pace		4	0:45		2	0:50		2	1:00		2	1:10

11

Set Type	Gold Set Dist	Gold Repeats	Gold Interval	Silver Set Dist	Silver Repeats	Silver Interval	SET	Bronze Set Dist	Bronze Repeats	Bronze Interval	Novice Set Dist	Novice Repeats	Novice Interval
Middle Distance	1050	2	2:55	950	2	3:15	200 sub 2:12 (2:25, 2:56, 3:18) neg split	750	1	3:55	650	1	4:25
		4	1:30		4	1:20	125 (S=100) Strong		4	2:00		3	2:15
		6	0:27		6	0:30	25 Back		4	0:35		3	0:40
	1150	2	3:20	1050	2	3:40	250 Neg Split	900	2	4:25	800	2	5:00
		3	2:00		3	2:10	150 Cruise		2	2:40		1	3:00
		4	0:40		2	0:45	50 Build		2	0:55		3	1:00
	1200	3	250	1100	3	250	r:05 Sub 2:55, 3:10, 3:04, 3:28	850	2	200	750	2	200
		3	100		2	100	r:05 Sub 1:10, 1:16, 1:32, 1:44		3	100		2	100
		3	50		3	50	r:05 Sub 35, 38, 46, 52		3	50		3	50
Speed	750	4	0:30	650	4	0:30	25 odds: Kick evens: Drill	500	3	0:40	500	3	0:45
		4	0:20		4	0:25	25 Dead Sprints		3	0:30		3	0:30
		3	0:40		3	0:50	50 Blast		2	0:55		2	1:00
		2	1:00		2	1:10	75 Fast		1	1:20		1	1:30
		3	0:40		2	0:50	50 Blast		2	0:55		2	1:00
		4	0:20		2	0:25	25 Dead Sprints		3	0:30		3	0:30
	750	14	0:30	700	12	0:30	25 {2=BLAST ; 1=1 breath ; 1=EZ} rotate	600	8	0:35	550	7	0:40
		4	0:45		4	0:50	25 EZ Not Free		4	0:55		3	1:05
		1	0:35		1	0:40	50 Each 50 Gets Faster		1	0:50		1	0:55
		2	0:40		2	0:45	50 | |		2	0:55		2	1:00
		3	0:45		3	0:50	50 V V		3	1:00		3	1:05
	900	12	0:30	800	12	0:35	25 3:Drill 1:Sprint	700	8	0:40	600	8	0:45
		6	1:15		5	1:20	100 aim for 10sec rest		5	1:40		4	1:55

12

Under 15 Minutes

Set Type	Gold Set Dist	Gold Repeats	Gold Interval	Silver Set Dist	Silver Repeats	Silver Interval	SET	Bronze Set Dist	Bronze Repeats	Bronze Interval	Novice Set Dist	Novice Repeats	Novice Interval
Speed	1000	10	1:15	900	9	1:25	100's at the below paces	800	8	1:45	700	7	1:55
		{4	@1:10		{3	@1:17	Pace		{3	@1:33		{2	@1:45
		{3	@1:07		{3	@1:13	Pace		{2	@1:29		{2	@1:40
		{2	@1:04		{2	@1:10	Pace		{2	@1:25		{2	@1:36
		{1	@1:01		{1	@1:07	Or Max Effort		{1	@1:21		{1	@1:31
	1000	-	-	950	1	0:50	50's Kick/Build x25	750	3	1:00	700	4	1:15
		5x			4x		Speed Play		3x			2x	
		{4	0:25		{4	0:30	25's Just Make It		{4	0:35		{5	0:35
		{4	==>		{4	==>	25's WIND IT UP Rd 1@22, Rd2@20, Rd3@18, Rd4@16, Rd5@14		{4	==>		{5	==>
Short Rest Interval	900	4	1:45	800	4	1:55	125 sub 1:20 (1:28, 1:47, 2:00)	650	2	2:20	550	2	2:40
		3	0:50		3	0:55	50 IM order		3	1:05		3	1:15
		5	0:35		3	0:40	50 @31 (34, 41, 46)		5	0:45		3	0:55
	1050	3	2:40	850	2	3:00	200 Pull steady	700	2	3:35	700	2	4:00
		1	0:50		1	0:55	A&B=75's C&D=50's Touch & Go		1	0:45		1	0:50
		2	0:55		2	1:00	A&B=75's C&D=50's Shoot for 5sec Rest		2	0:50		2	0:55
		3	1:00		3	1:05	A&B=75's C&D=50's Shoot for 10sec Rest		3	0:55		3	1:00
Stroke	1200	2x {4	1:15	1100	2x {4	1:20	{100 FAST	900	2x {3	1:40	800	2x {2	1:55
		{1	2:30		{1	2:05	{200 BC 5-3 x50 (S&B=150)		{1	2:30		{1	3:50
	600	16	0:30	500	12	0:35	25 IM order	450	12	0:40	400	12	0:45
		4	1:00		4	1:10	50 Under/Overs		3	1:20		2	1:30
	750	6	0:50	700	5	0:55	50 Not Free	600	3	1:05	550	2	1:15
		1	5:50		1	6:25	450 of 25BLAST/50EZ, BLAST is Race Stroke		1	7:40		1	8:45
	950	6	1:50	900	6	2:00	125 25Fly / 75Fr/ 25IM Order	700	4	2:30	650	4	2:45
		4	0:45		3	0:50	50 ALL OUT		4	1:00		3	1:10

Set Type	Gold Set Dist	Gold Repeats	Gold Interval	Silver Set Dist	Silver Repeats	Silver Interval	SET	Bronze Set Dist	Bronze Repeats	Bronze Interval	Novice Set Dist	Novice Repeats	Novice Interval
Distance	1250	2	300	1150	2	275	3:45 Cruise	950	2	225	850	2	200
		2	0:55		2	1:00	75 @ 45 (49, 1:00, 1:07)		2	1:15		2	1:15
		1	500		1	450	6:15 Steady		1	350		1	300
	1300	1	7:30	1250	1	8:15	600 Pull	950	1	10:00	900	1	11:15
		2	3:05		2	3:25	250 Steady		1	4:05		1	4:35
		4	0:45		3	0:50	50 Bk		3	1:00		2	1:10
	1500	1	6:20	1400	1	5:30	500 (S=400, B=150) hold 1:15 (1:22, 1:40)	1150	1	2:30	1000	1	–
		1	5:05		1	5:30	400 hold 1:13 (1:20, 1:37, 1:49)		1	6:45		1	7:40
		1	3:50		1	4:10	300 hold 1:11 (1:18, 1:34, 1:46)		1	5:05		1	5:45
		1	2:35		1	2:50	200 hold 1:09 (1:16, 1:31, 1:43)		1	3:25		1	3:55
		1	1:20		1	1:30	100 hold 1:07 (1:14, 1:28, 1:40)		1	1:45		1	2:00
	1600	2	5:45	1500	2	6:15	500 (B&N=400)	1200	2	6:10	1100	2	6:55
		R	0:10		R	0:10	REST (put on fins)		R	0:10		R	0:10
		12	0:35		10	0:35	50 w/ Fins		8	0:45		6	0:50
General	1000	4	1:05	850	2	1:10	75 sub50 (0:55, 1:07, 1:15)	750	2	1:25	700	2	1:40
		2	2:10		2	2:25	150 desc		2	2:55		2	3:15
		6	0:35		6	0:40	25 o:Kick e:Drill NF		4	0:45		4	0:50
		5	0:55		5	1:00	50 2:Fl/Bk 1:Bk/Br 2:Br/Fr		4	1:15		3	1:25
	1100	10	0:50	1000	8	0:55	50's Double Turn (start from center of pool)	800	8	1:05	700	6	1:15
		R	0:15		R	0:15	GET TO THE WALL		R	0:15		R	0:30
		3	2:45		3	3:00	200 Pull		2	3:40		2	4:10
	1100	5	1:30	1000	5	1:40	100 1-2:Steady 3-5:Desc	950	4	2:00	750	4	2:15
		8	0:50		7	0:55	50 IM Order		7	1:05		5	1:15
		8	0:25		6	0:30	25 Drill LAST 2-->1:Sprint 2:Underwater		8	0:35		4	0:35
	1150	10	0:45	1050	8	0:50	50 1,6:Cruise 2-4, 7-10: sub30 (33, 40, 45)	900	8	1:00	800	6	1:05
		2	1:30		2	1:40	100 Breath Control 5		2	2:00		2	2:15
		1	8:00		1	8:50	450 (B&N=300) Kick Pyramid (25Fast/25EZ/25EZ/50Fast/50EZ/ 75Fast/75EZ/50Fast/50EZ/25Fast/25EZ)		1	7:00		1	8:00

Set Type	SET	Set Dist (Gold)	Gold Reps	Gold Int	Set Dist (Silver)	Silver Reps	Silver Int	Set Dist (Bronze)	Bronze Reps	Bronze Int	Set Dist (Novice)	Novice Reps	Novice Int
General	100 @ 1:10 (1:16, 1:33, 1:45)	1150	4	1:15	1050	4	1:20	850	3	1:40	750	3	1:55
	50 bk		1	0:55		1	1:00		1	1:05		1	1:25
	100 @ 1:15 (1:21, 1:39, 1:52)		3	1:20		3	1:25		2	1:45		2	2:00
	50 bk		1	0:55		1	1:00		1	1:05		1	1:25
	100 @ 1:20 (1:28, 1:46, 2:00)		2	1:25		2	1:35		1	1:50		1	2:05
	50 bk		1	0:55		1	1:00		1	1:05		1	1:25
	100 EZ		1	1:30		1	-		1	2:00		-	-
	50 build to 500 pace	1150	2	0:40	1100	1	0:45	900	1	0:50	750	1	1:00
	50 EZ		1	1:00		1	1:05		1	1:20		1	1:30
	100 build to above 500 pace		2	1:20		2	1:25		2	1:45		2	2:00
	50 EZ		1	1:00		1	1:05		1	1:20		1	1:30
	150 Build to max pace		2	2:00		2	2:10		2	2:40		1	3:00
	50 EZ		1	1:00		1	1:05		1	1:20		1	1:30
	200 Build to strong		2	2:40		1	2:55		1	3:30		1	4:00
	{3:30 Kick	1200	2x {1	200	1050	2x {1	175	900	2x {1	150	800	2x {1	150
	{2:40 Swim Strong		{2	200		{2	175		{2	150		{2	125
	{100 BC 5-3 x50	1200	3x {3	1:20	1100	2x {4	1:30	900	2x {3	1:45	800	2x {3	2:00
	{50 Build		{2	0:45		{3	0:50		{3	1:00		{2	1:10
	300 Negative Split	1200	1	3:45	1100	1	4:10	900	1	5:00	850	1	5:40
	200 Pull Descend		2	2:35		2	2:50		3	3:25		1	3:55
	100 Mix in 25 sprint (you pick)		3	1:15		3	1:25		3	1:40		2	1:55
	50 Kick		4	0:55		2	1:00		2	1:15		3	1:15
	50 build each 25 to race pace	1250	10	0:45	1100	7	0:50	950	6	1:00	850	4	1:10
	100 build each 50 to faster than Race Pace		5	1:25		5	1:30		4	1:50		4	2:05
	50 bk		1	1:00		1	1:05		1	1:20		1	1:30
	200 @1:09 (1:15, 1:31, 1:44)		1	2:30		1	2:45		1	3:20		1	3:45
	200 Cruise	1300	5	2:30	1150	4	2:45	1000	4	3:20	850	3	3:45
	50 odds:EZ evens:FAST		6	1:00		7	1:05		4	1:20		5	1:30

Set Type	Gold Set Dist	Gold Repeats	Gold Interval	Silver Set Dist	Silver Repeats	Silver Interval	SET	Bronze Set Dist	Bronze Repeats	Bronze Interval	Novice Set Dist	Novice Repeats	Novice Interval
General	1300	2x {2	2:05	1200	2x {2	2:20	{150 50fast, 100cruise (B=125)	900	2x {2	2:20	800	2x {1	3:10
		{2	1:20		{2	1:30	{100 Perfect Stroke		{1	2:00		{1	2:00
		{3	0:55		{2	1:00	{50 rd1:Fly rd:2IM rotation		{2	1:15		{3	1:25
	1300	4	1:50	1200	4	2:00	150 Descend	600	2	2:25	800	2	2:45
		8	0:55		6	1:00	50 IM order/Sx25		6	1:15		4	1:30
		4	1:15		4	1:25	75 2:Strong 2:Fast		4	1:40		4	1:55
	1300	5	1:20	1200	5	1:27	100 Cruise	950	4	1:50	600	4	2:00
		8	0:40		6	0:45	50 EZ (choice of strokes)		5	0:55		4	1:00
		4	1:18		4	1:25	100 Distance Per Stroke (relax)		3	1:45		3	1:55
	1300	4	1:20	1200	3	1:25	100 BC7	1000	3	1:45	600	4	2:00
		4	2:40		4	2:55	200 75Build/25EZ x2		3	3:30		2	4:00
		4	0:20		4	0:25	25 Heads Up		4	0:30		4	0:30
	1300	10	0:42	1200	8	0:45	50 Steady	1000	8	0:55	600	10	1:00
		4	2:55		4	3:10	200 IM		3	3:50		2	4:30
	1300	5	1:30	1200	4	1:40	100 Descend	1000	3	2:00	950	3	2:15
		6	0:45		6	0:50	50 Drill/Build		4	1:00		3	1:05
		1	6:15		1	6:50	500 alt 100@1:05/100EZ		1	8:20		1	9:00
	1350	3x {3	1:15	1200	3x {3	1:25	FINS {100 S	900	3x {2	1:40	900	3x {2	1:50
		{6	0:30		{4	0:35	{25 Underwater Kick		{4	0:40		{4	0:45
	1350	5	1:30	1200	5	1:40	100 Last 3 Descend	1050	5	2:00	600	4	2:15
		6	0:45		4	0:50	50 25EZ/25Build		2	1:00		2	1:05
		2	0:25		2	0:25	25 Drill		2	0:30		2	0:35
		1	500		1	450	6:20 alt100FAST/100Cruise (not EZ)		1	400		1	350
	1400	4	0:50	1250	4	0:55	50 Overkick	1100	3	1:00	950	3	1:10
		R	0:15		R	0:15	R0:15 Put on Equipment		R	0:15		R	0:15
		8	1:15		8	1:20	100 w/ Fins (optional Paddles)		7	1:40		6	1:50
		16	0:25		10	0:30	25 IM order w/ Fins, Breast use dolphin kick		10	0:30		8	0:35

16

15-20 Minutes

Set Type	SET	Gold Set Dist	Gold Repeats	Gold Interval	Silver Set Dist	Silver Repeats	Silver Interval	Bronze Set Dist	Bronze Repeats	Bronze Interval	Novice Set Dist	Novice Repeats	Novice Interval
General	{300 NegSp&Desc (N=250)	1400	2x {2	3:50	1400	2x {2	4:00	1100	1x {3	5:05	950	1x {3	4:50
	{100 IM		{1	1:50		{1	1:50		{2	2:25		{2	2:45
	75 Right arm only/Left arm only/ Build Swim x25	1450	6	1:10	1300	4	1:20	1050	4	1:30	900	4	1:45
	125 Best Average, Last 2 Sprint last 50 (N=100)		8	1:35		8	1:45		6	2:05		6	1:55
	200 Descend	1600	4	2:35	1400	3	2:50	950	2	3:25	850	2	3:55
	75 #1-50Fly/25Bk #2-25Fly/Bk/Br {#3-50Bk/25Br #4-Bk/Br/Fr <B&N do #3&4>		4	1:15		4	1:25		2	1:40		2	1:55
	100 1,2:Steady, 3-5:Desc to Max Effort	1200	5	1:15	1400	5	1:25	900	4	1:40	850	3	1:55
Middle Distance	50 build each 25 (steady down, strong back)	1200	10	0:45	1050	9	0:50	900	6	1:00	850	5	1:05
	100 build		5	1:30		4	1:40		4	2:00		4	2:15
	200 @1:10 (1:17, 1:33, 1:45) smooth		1	2:30		1	2:45		1	3:20		1	3:45
	100 Just Make It	1200	4	1:13	1100	3	1:20	900	2	1:37	800	2	1:50
	300 BLAST (N=200 BLAST)		1	5:45		1	6:20		1	7:40		1	5:40
	100 Just Make It		3	1:15		3	1:23		2	1:40		2	1:55
	200 BLAST		1	2:35		1	2:50		1	3:20		1	3:45
	100 @ 1:05 (1:11, 1:26, 1:37) pace	1200	4	1:30	1100	4	1:40	900	3	2:00	800	3	2:15
	400 REALLY EZ (C&D = 300)		1	5:30		1	6:00		1	5:30		1	6:10
	100 @ 1:05 (1:11, 1:26, 1:37) pace		4	1:30		3	1:40		3	2:00		2	2:15
	100 Cruise	1250	5	1:15	1150	4	1:20	1000	4	1:40	850	4	1:55
	50 IM rot		9	0:55		9	1:00		6	1:10		3	1:25
	300 Fast		1	4:00		1	4:25		1	5:00		1	6:00
	r:15 neg. split each swim	1300	1	100	1200	1	100	1000	1	100	900	1	100
	r:15 Descend pace of each effort		1	300		1	250		1	200		1	200
	r:15		1	500		1	500		1	400		1	300
	r:15		1	300		1	250		1	200		1	200
	r:15		1	100		1	100		1	100		1	100

15-20 Minutes

Set Type	Gold			Silver			SET	Bronze			Novice	
	Set Dist	Repeats	Interval	Set Dist	Repeats	Interval		Set Dist	Repeats	Interval	Repeats	Interval
Middle Distance	1450	1	3:45	1350	1	4:10	300 Build each 50 (B&N=200)	1150	1	3:15	1	3:50
		2	2:30		2	2:45	200 Neg Split		2	3:15	2	3:50
		6	1:25		5	1:35	100 1st 25 not free, last 75 BLAST Free		4	1:55	3	2:05
		1	2:00		1	2:10	150 Build each 25 (N=100)		1	2:40	1	2:00
	1500	3	2:35	1300	2	2:50	200 Cruise (N=150)	1100	1	3:25	2	2:55
		1	2:50		1	3:05	200 FAST (N=150)		1	3:45	1	3:15
		2	2:35		2	2:50	200 Cruise (N=150)		2	3:25	2	2:55
		1	1:25		1	1:35	100 FAST		1	1:55	1	2:05
		1	2:35		1	2:50	200 Cruise (N=150)		1	3:25	1	2:55
	1500	4	1:15	1400	4	1:20	100	1100	3	1:40	2	1:55
		4	0:38		4	0:40	50		4	0:50	4	0:55
		5	1:17		4	1:25	100		3	1:42	3	2:00
		1	4:55		1	5:15	400 (B&N=300) Pace sub1:10 (1:17,1:33, 1:45)		1	4:55	1	5:30
	1500	5	1:25	1400	4	1:30	100 (25Drill/75Swim)	1200	2	1:45	4	2:05
		4	1:20		4	1:25	100		4	1:40	3	1:55
		3	1:15		3	1:20	100		3	1:35	2	1:50
		2	1:10		2	1:15	100		2	1:30	1	1:45
		1	1:05		1	1:10	100		1	1:25	1	-
Speed	1000	2x		900	2x			800	2x		2x	
		{2	1:55		{2	2:05	{125 (B&N=100) sub1:24 (1:32, 1:30, 1:40)		{2	2:00	{2	2:10
		{6	0:35		{4	0:40	{25 1-3:Not Free 4-6:Fr 3&6:Build		{4	0:45	{2	1:00
		{2	1:00		{2	1:05	{50 sub30 (33, 40, 45)		{2	1:20	{2	1:30
	1000	10	1:45	900	9	1:55	100's	800	8	2:20	7	2:35
							<==Evens: Breath Control 5					
							Odds: FAST					
			1:30			1:35	#1			1:50		2:00
			1:25			1:30	#3			1:45		1:55
			1:20			1:25	#5			1:40		1:50
			1:15			1:20	#7			1:35		1:45
			1:10			1:15	#9			-		-

Set Type	SET	Gold Set Dist	Gold Repeats	Gold Interval	Silver Set Dist	Silver Repeats	Silver Interval	Bronze Set Dist	Bronze Repeats	Bronze Interval	Novice Set Dist	Novice Repeats	Novice Interval
Speed	100 Descend	1050	5	1:20	950	4	1:30	800	4	1:45	700	3	2:00
	75 of 25 Free/25 Not Free/25 Free		4	1:05		4	1:10		3	1:25		2	1:35
	50 sub 31 (34, 41, 0:46)		3	0:45		3	0:50		3	1:00		3	1:05
	25 #1:EZ Not Free #2-4:Sprint Free		4	0:35		4	0:40		4	0:45		4	0:50
	75 last 25 Fast (optional - Zoomers/Fins)	1100	12	1:00	950	10	1:10	800	8	1:20	650	6	1:30
	100 EZ		1	2:00		1	2:15		1	2:40		1	3:00
	25 DEAD SPRINT		4	0:40		4	0:40		4	0:50		4	1:00
	75 Cruise (N=50) 2x		4	1:05		2	1:10		4	1:25		2	1:05
	{25 Build 2x	1100	{4	0:20	950	{4	0:22	900	{3	0:25	700	{3	0:30
	{25 Off the Blocks		{4	0:30		{4	0:33		{3	0:35		{3	0:45
	{25 Sprint		{4	0:20		{4	0:22		{3	0:25		{3	0:30
	{25 EZ		{4	0:25		{4	0:28		{3	0:30		{3	0:40
	300 #1-Build #2 EZ (B&N=225)	1100	2	4:00	1000	2	4:25	850	2	4:00	750	2	4:30
	100 ALL OUT (Choice of stroke)		5	1:30		4	1:35		4	2:00		3	2:15
	200 Build each 50	1100	1	2:35	1000	1	2:50	800	1	3:25	700	1	3:50
	100 Descend		3	1:35		2	1:45		2	2:05		2	2:20
	100 Sprint last 25		2	1:30		2	1:40		2	2:00		2	2:15
	100 25Fly/75Cruise		2	1:25		2	1:35		1	1:55		-	-
	50 sub31 (34, 41, 46)		3	0:55		3	1:00		3	1:15		3	1:20
	25 Sprint		2	0:40		2	0:45		-	-		-	-
	200 Build 50's	1150	1	2:40	1050	1	2:55	850	1	3:35	750	1	4:00
	100 Desc 1-3		3	1:30		3	1:40		3	2:00		3	2:15
	50 Bk		1	1:00		1	1:05		1	1:20		1	1:30
	100 Sprint last 25		2	1:30		1	1:40		1	2:00		-	-
	100 25Fly/75Cruise		2	1:25		1	1:35		-	-		-	-
	50 sub31 (34, 41, 46)		3	0:50		3	0:55		3	1:10		3	1:15
	25 Sprint		2	0:40		2	0:45		2	0:50		2	1:00

Set Type	Gold Set Dist	Gold Repeats	Gold Interval	Silver Set Dist	Silver Repeats	Silver Interval	SET	Bronze Set Dist	Bronze Repeats	Bronze Interval	Novice Set Dist	Novice Repeats	Novice Interval
Speed	1200	8x {4	=>	1050	7x {4	=>	{25 Just make it :-) {rd1=28 rd2=26, rd3=24,	900	5x {4	=>	800	4x {4	=>
		{2	0:35		{2	0:45	{rd4=22, rd5=20, rd6=18, rd7=16, rd8=14		{2	0:55		{2	1:00
			-			-	{25 #1-Kick on back #2-Drill		3	1:05		4	1:15
							50 GOLF (add strokes + time) desc score						
Speed	1200	4x {4	0:35	1200	4x {4	0:38	50 FAST	900	3x {4	0:45	750	3x {3	0:50
		{1	2:40		{1	2:30	100 EZ		{1	3:40		{1	4:00
Speed	1300	4	1:25	1200	4	1:30	100 Goal for the set is 10 sec rest on each swim	1000	3	1:45	900	3	1:55
		3	1:20		3	1:25	100		2	1:40		2	1:50
		2	1:15		2	1:20	100		2	1:35		1	1:45
		1	1:10		1	1:15	100		1	1:30		1	1:50
		1	1:15		1	1:20	100		1	1:35		1	1:55
		1	1:20		1	1:25	100		1	1:40		1	2:00
		1	1:25			-	100			-			-
Short Rest Interval	1250	3	0:40	1150	3	0:45	50 Build	950	3	0:50	850	3	1:00
		2	0:35		2	0:40	50		2	0:45		2	0:55
		1	0:30		1	0:35	50 Fast		1	0:40		1	0:50
		6	0:50		5	0:55	50 25Choice/25Free		6	1:05		4	1:15
		3	1:10		2	1:15	50 Kick		2	1:30		2	1:45
		4	1:35		4	1:45	125 of 50 Build / 50Strong / Rest:05 / 25Sprint		2	2:05		2	2:25
Short Rest Interval	1300	4	1:15	1200	4	1:23	100 Cruise	1000	3	1:40	900	3	1:55
		8	0:40		8	0:45	50 Blast		6	0:55		4	1:00
		5	1:12		4	1:20	100 Strong		4	1:35		4	1:50
Short Rest Interval	1300	6	1:55	1200	6	2:05	150 Descend by 5 sec	1000	6	2:30	900	6	2:50
		4	1:25		3	1:35	100 25EZ/50IMo/25Strong		1	1:55			-
Short Rest Interval	1400	8	1:15	1300	7	1:20	100 Make it by 5 sec	1000	5	1:40	900	5	1:55
		4	1:10		4	1:15	100 |		3	1:35		3	1:45
		2	1:05		2	1:10	100 V		2	1:30		1	1:40

Set Type	SET	Gold Set Dist	Gold Rep	Gold Int	Silver Set Dist	Silver Rep	Silver Int	Bronze Set Dist	Bronze Rep	Bronze Int	Novice Set Dist	Novice Rep	Novice Int
Short Rest Interval	200 (B&N=150)		4	2:30		4	2:45		4	2:30		3	2:50
	50		4	0:35		4	0:40		4	0:45		4	0:50
	100 (B&N=75)		4	1:15		3	1:22		4	1:15		4	1:25
	Set Dist	**1400**			**1300**			**1100**			**950**		
	50 Make it		5	0:35		5	0:38		4	0:45		3	0:50
	100 Negative Split		5	1:15		4	1:20		4	1:40		3	1:50
	200 Last 25 Fast		2	2:35		2	2:50		2	3:25		1	3:55
	100 Build		2	1:15		2	1:20		2	1:40		2	1:50
	50 Faster than 1st 50's		2	0:37		2	0:40		2	0:48		2	0:55
	Set Dist	**1450**			**1350**			**1100**			**950**		
	125 100Steady / r:05 / 25 Sprint		6	1:30		5	1:40		4	2:00		4	2:15
	25 EZ Choice		3	0:40		3	0:45		3	0:50		2	1:00
	75 50Strong / r:10 / 25 Sprint		6	1:00		5	1:10		4	1:20		4	1:30
	25 EZ Choice		3	0:40		3	0:45		2	0:50		2	1:00
	25 Fast		6	0:17		6	0:19		7	0:23		4	0:25
	Set Dist	**1500**			**1300**			**1100**			**1000**		
	Build every 3rd 25	300	on	4:00	225	on	3:30	250	on	4:30	250	on	2:15
	75 Cruise		3	1:05		3	1:10		3	1:25		3	1:35
	75 Strong		2	0:58		2	1:03		2	1:15		2	1:25
	75 Fast		1	0:50		1	0:55		1	1:05		1	1:15
	50 Cruise		3	0:38		3	0:42		3	0:50		3	1:00
	50 Strong		2	0:35		2	0:38		2	0:45		2	0:55
	50 Fast		1	0:31		1	0:33		1	0:40		1	0:50
	25 Cruise		3	0:23		3	0:25		3	0:30		3	0:35
	25 Strong		2	0:19		2	0:21		2	0:25		2	0:30
	25 Fast		1	0:15		1	0:17		1	0:20		1	0:25
	Set Dist	**1500**			**1350**			**1150**			**1000**		
	100 Just Make it		2	1:15		1	1:25		3	1:40		2	1:55
	200 ___		1	2:25		1	2:40		1	3:10		1	3:40
	300 ___		1	3:35		1	3:55		1	4:40		1	5:25
	400 ___		1	4:45		1	5:10		1	6:10		1	7:10
	500 V V		1	5:55		1	6:25		-	-		-	-
	Set Dist	**1600**			**1500**			**1200**			**1100**		

15-20 Minutes

Set Type	Gold Set Dist	Gold Repeats	Gold Interval	Silver Set Dist	Silver Repeats	Silver Interval	SET	Bronze Set Dist	Bronze Repeats	Bronze Interval	Novice Set Dist	Novice Repeats	Novice Interval
SRI	1650	2	300	1450	2	275	3:50 #1-Moderate #2-Strong	1200	2	225	1000	2	200
		3	175		3	150	2:10		3	125		3	100
		2	175		2	150	2:00		2	125		2	100
		1	175		1	150	1:50 This must be fast to make interval		1	125		1	100
	1150	2	1:55	1000	2	2:05	150 Build	850	1	2:35	800	1	2:55
		3	1:30		3	1:40	100 (B&N=75) @1:03 (1:09, 1:03, 1:10)		3	1:30		3	1:40
		2	1:30		2	1:40	75 EZ Not Free		1	2:00		1	2:15
		2	1:40		2	1:50	100 1st50 Not Free Drill / 50Swim		2	2:15		2	2:30
		4	0:55		4	1:00	50 Not Free BLAST		4	1:15		3	1:15
	1200	4	2:15	1050	3	2:30	150 Choice	900	2	3:00	750	1	3:45
		1	10:00		1	11:00	600 Bk-Br-Fr x25		1	13:00		1	15:00
Stroke	1450	1	4:20	1350	1	4:45	325 Last 25 Sprint Back	1100	–	–	900	–	–
		1	3:00		1	3:20	225 Last 25 Sprint Breast		1	4:00		1	4:45
		2	1:40		2	1:50	125 Last 25 Sprint Fly		1	2:15		1	2:45
		1	3:00		1	3:20	225 Last 25 Sprint Back		1	4:00		1	4:45
		1	4:20		1	4:45	325 Last 25 Sprint Breast		1	5:45		1	6:45
		1	1:30		–	–	100 IM		2	2:00		–	–
	1200	6	1:50	1000	4	2:05	100 IM	900	4	2:20	800	3	2:35
		24	0:25		24	0:30	25 Sets of 4 {1-3:Drills 4:Sprint} (1-4, 9-12, 17-20 = Choice | 5-8, 13-16, 21-24 = Not Free)		20	0:35		20	0:40
	1300	1	3:00	1200	1	3:15	200 Bk (N=150)	1000	1	4:00	900	1	3:25
		1	3:30		1	3:50	200 Drill Stroke (NOT FREE) (N=150)		1	4:30		1	3:55
		5	0:50		5	0:55	50 Kick/Swim (NOT FREE)		3	1:05		3	1:10
		4	1:35		3	1:45	100 Build (NOT FREE)		3	2:05		3	2:25
		5	0:40		5	0:45	50 o:FAST e:EZ Choice		3	0:50		3	1:00

15-20 Minutes

22

Set Type		Gold			Silver			SET	Bronze			Novice		
		Set Dist	Repeats	Interval	Set Dist	Repeats	Interval		Set Dist	Repeats	Interval	Set Dist	Repeats	Interval
Distance		1300	8	0:45	1200	6	0:50	50 Cruise	1050	6	1:00	900	5	1:05
			1	5:30		1	6:00	400 FAST (N=300)		1	7:20		1	6:10
			12	0:30		12	0:35	25 4:Br 4:Bk 4:Fly		6	0:40		6	0:45
			4	0:45		4	0:50	50 sub30 (33, 40, 45)		4	1:00		4	1:05
		1500	3	3:55	1350	3	4:20	300 Desc 1-3 (B&N=200)	1250	3	3:25	1000	3	3:55
			2	1:00		2	1:05	50 EZ		2	1:20		1	1:30
			4	1:15		2	1:25	75 50stk/25S		2	1:40		2	1:55
			R	0:30		R	0:30	R0:30		R	0:30		-	-
			1	2:45		1	3:00	200 ALL OUT		1	3:40		1	4:00
		1700	2	6:00	1550	2	6:40	500 aim5:55 (6:35, 7:55, 8:50)	1400	2	8:00	1150	1	9:00
			2	2:25		2	2:40	200 aim2:20 (3:35, 3:00, 3:30)		1	3:05		2	3:40
			2	1:15		1	1:25	100 aim1:10 (1:20, 1:35, 1:45)		1	1:40		2	1:55
			2	0:40		1	0:45	50 aim35 (40, 50, 52)		2	0:55		1	1:00
		1700	1	4:00	1600	1	4:25	300 50 Sprint, 25 Recover	1250	1	5:20	1100	1	6:00
			1	12:30		1	13:45	1000 Strong n Long (B=650, N=500)		1	10:50		1	9:40
			1	4:00		1	4:25	300 50 Sprint, 25 Recover		1	5:20		1	6:00
			1	1:15		-	-	100 Overkick		-	-		-	-
		1750	2	1:10	1650	2	1:20	75 Right arm only/Left arm only/Swim x25	1350	2	1:30	1150	2	1:45
			1	2:00		1	2:10	100 BK EZ		1	2:40		1	3:00
			1	5:50		1	6:25	500 @1:05's (1:11, 1:27)		1	7:40		1	8:45
			10	1:20		9	1:25	100 @1:04 (1:10, 1:25)		6	1:40		4	2:00
		1800	2	5:00	1700	2	5:30	400 (B&N=300) Descend	1400	2	5:00	1200	2	5:35
			10	1:15		9	1:20	100 1-6 Steady 7-10 Descend		8	1:40		6	1:55
Gen		1200	6	1:45	1100	5	1:55	100 streamline kick w/ fins	950	5	2:10	950	5	2:10
			8	1:30		8	1:40	75 MAX effort w/Paddles & Fins		6	2:00		6	2:00

20-25 Minutes

Set Type	\<Gold\> Set Dist	Repeats	Interval	\<Silver\> Set Dist	Repeats	Interval	SET	\<Bronze\> Set Dist	Repeats	Interval	\<Novice\> Set Dist	Repeats	Interval
General	1350	4	2:30	1200	3	2:45	150 ALL OUT	1000	3	3:20	900	3	3:45
		5	1:30		5	1:40	100 75Fr/25Bk		4	2:00		3	2:15
		3	1:45		3	1:55	75 IM ALL OUT		2	2:20		2	2:35
		1	1:00		1	1:05	25 Underwater		-	0:00		-	-
	1350	1	3:50	1200	1	4:15	300 Cruise	1050	1	5:10	900	1	5:40
		4	0:55		3	1:00	50 Br		3	1:15		2	1:25
		2	1:55		2	2:15	150 Cruise		2	2:35		2	2:50
		4	0:50		3	1:00	50 Bk		3	1:15		2	1:15
		4	1:00		4	1:10	75 Cruise		2	1:20		2	1:30
		4	0:50		3	1:00	50 Fly		3	1:15		2	1:15
	1400	5	0:45	1300	4	0:50	50 odds: Drill evens: Build	1000	3	1:00	900	3	1:05
		5	1:25		5	1:35	100 Pull		4	1:55		3	2:05
		5	0:45		4	0:50	50 Drill/Build x25		3	1:00		3	1:05
		5	0:55		5	1:05	50 Kick		4	1:15		3	1:20
		2	1:10		2	1:25	75 Back		2	1:35		2	1:45
	1400 2x	{1	2:35	1300 2x	{1	2:50	{200 Neg Split	1100 2x	{1	3:25	1000 2x	{1	3:55
		{4	1:00		{4	1:05	{50 Streamline Kick		{3	1:20		{2	1:30
		{4	0:45		{3	0:50	{50 Pull		{2	1:00		{2	1:05
		{1	1:25		{1	1:35	{100 Swim		{1	1:55		{1	2:05
	1450	1	3:15	1400	1	3:35	250 Swim (N=200)	1150	1	4:20	1050	1	3:55
		2	2:05		2	2:15	150 Build 50's		1	3:25		1	3:10
		4	1:20		4	1:30	100 last 2 sub 1:05 (1:12, 1:27, 1:38)		4	1:45		4	2:00
		8	0:35		6	0:40	25 Kick		5	0:45		3	0:50
		4	1:15		4	1:25	75 50stroke/25 Swim		3	1:40		3	1:50

Set Type	Gold Set Dist	Gold Repeats	Gold Interval	Silver Set Dist	Silver Repeats	Silver Interval	SET	Bronze Set Dist	Bronze Repeats	Bronze Interval	Novice Set Dist	Novice Repeats	Novice Interval
General	1500	4	2:50	1350	4	3:05	200 last 2 sub 2:12 (2:25, 2:56, 3:18)	1150	3	3:45	1000	3	4:15
		12	0:30		10	0:35	25 Streamline Kick		10	0:40		10	0:45
		8	0:45		6	0:50	50 Back		6	1:00		3	1:10
		2x			2x				2x			1x	
	1500	{1	3:05	1400	{1	3:25	250 Build by 50	1000	-	-	1000	{2	4:35
		{1	4:20		{1	4:45	350 Pull (Long Strokes)		{1	5:45		{1	6:30
		{2	1:00		{1	1:05	50 Free/Bk x25		{2	1:20		{2	1:30
		{2	0:30		{2	0:35	25 SPRINT		{2	0:40		{2	0:45
	1500	8	1:30	1400	7	1:40	100 cruise	1150	6	2:00	1050	6	2:10
		4	1:15		4	1:25	75 Bk		2	1:40		2	1:55
		2	2:40		2	2:55	200 cruise (N=150)		2	3:35		2	3:05
	1500	4	1:55	1400	4	2:05	150 build last 50	1200	4	2:35	1100	4	2:55
		8	0:50		6	0:55	50 Bk		5	1:05		3	1:15
		4	1:40		4	1:50	125 cruise		2	2:15		2	2:30
	1500	4	1:00	1400	4	1:00	50 25 Single arm Drill/25 Swim	1200	4	1:15	1100	2	1:20
		3	1:50		3	2:00	150 1-3:Descend 4:Last 50 Fast		4	2:25		4	2:40
		7	0:35		6	0:40	25 o:Choice e:Kick		4	0:45		4	0:50
		9	1:00		8	1:05	75 #1:Fast #2:EZ #3,4:Fast #5:EZ} Repeat		4	1:20		4	1:30
	1500	2	3:40	1400	2	4:00	300 Cruise (N=200)	1250	2	4:50	1000	2	3:40
		12	0:30		12	0:35	25 4:Br 4:Bk 4:Fly		9	0:40		9	0:45
		6	0:55		4	1:00	50 Not Free		4	1:10		3	1:25
		4	1:05		4	1:10	75 @47 (51, 1:03, 1:11)		3	1:20		3	1:40
		3x			2x				2x			2x	
	1500	{1	4:50	1500	{1	4:35	{350 (S=300, B=400) NegSp by 5+ sec	1100	{1	7:30	1000	{1	7:15
		{1	0:20		{1	0:25	{25 SPRINT		{1	0:30		{1	0:30
		{1	1:05		{1	1:10	{50 Drill EZ		{1	1:30		{1	1:40
		{1	1:05		{1	1:10	{75 50Build/25Sprint		{1	1:30		{1	1:40

Set Type	Gold Set Dist	Gold Repeats	Gold Interval	Silver Set Dist	Silver Repeats	Silver Interval	SET	Bronze Set Dist	Bronze Repeats	Bronze Interval	Novice Set Dist	Novice Repeats	Novice Interval
General	1600	2x		1400	2x			1200	2x		1100	2x	
		{1	2:45		{1	3:00	{200 Distance Per Stroke		{1	3:40		{1	4:10
		{2	1:25		{2	1:35	{100 BC 5 (N=75)		{2	1:55		{2	1:35
		{4	0:45		{4	0:50	{50 => 20yds EZ / 30yds Fast		{2	1:00		{2	1:05
		{8	0:25		{4	0:30	{25 Build		{4	0:35		{4	0:35
	1600	2x		1400	2x		2X	1200	2x		1000	2x	
		{2	2:40		{2	2:55	{200 EZ		{1	3:35		{1	4:00
		{4	==>		{3	==>	{100 rd1:Pull (G=1:20, S=1:30, B=1:50, N=2:00)		{4	==>		{3	==>
							{rd2:Kick (G=2:00, S=2:15, B=2:40, N=3:00)						
	1600	4	1:40	1400	4	1:50	125 FAST	1200	3	2:15	1100	3	2:30
		4	1:35		4	1:45	125 Cruise		3	2:05		3	2:25
		6	0:55		6	1:00	50 Not Free		5	1:15		3	1:25
		12	0:30		8	0:35	25 Every 3rd Sprint 1-6:Free 7-12:Not Free		8	0:40		8	0:45
	1650	6	2:25	1450	5	2:40	200 Steady (N=150)	1200	4	3:15	1050	5	2:45
		4	1:10		4	1:15	75 Bk/Br/Fly		4	1:35		2	1:45
		6	0:40		6	0:50	25 SPRINT		4	1:00		6	1:00
	1650	3	3:15	1450	3	3:35	250 build last 50	1200	2	4:20	1100	2	5:00
		16	0:30		12	0:35	25 4:Fly 1breath 4:Bk 7mUnder 4:Br 4:1Breath		12	0:40		8	0:45
		5	1:15		4	1:25	100 @1:05 (1:12, 1:27, 1:38)		4	1:40		4	2:00
	1650	8	1:15	1450	7	1:25	100 Steady Swim------Whole set w/ FINS	1300	6	1:40	1200	6	1:50
		8	0:30		8	0:35	25 Underwater		6	0:40		4	0:40
		R	0:30		R	0:30	R0:30		R	0:30		R	0:30
		2	2:40		2	2:55	200 Steady		2	3:35		2	4:00
		9	0:30		6	0:35	25 #1:2 #2:1 #3:0 Breaths per 25		6	0:40		3	0:40
		1	1:00		-	-	25 Underwater		-	-		1	0:50
	1650	5	3:05	1500	4	3:25	250 Strong rotate through 50 not free (N=200)	1200	4	4:10	1000	4	4:00
		4	1:20		5	1:30	100		2	1:45		2	2:00

Set Type	Gold			Silver			SET	Bronze			Novice		
	Set Dist	Repeats	Interval	Set Dist	Repeats	Interval		Set Dist	Repeats	Interval	Set Dist	Repeats	Interval
General		5	0:40		5	0:40	50 Focus on driving kick		4	0:55		2	1:00
		3	1:15		3	1:20	100 Fast arms		2	1:40		2	2:00
		2	2:35		2	2:50	200 Long strong		2	3:45		2	4:00
	1650	7	1:20	1550	6	1:25	100 Descend	1200	4	1:45	1100	4	2:00
		6	2:25		5	2:40	200 3rd 50 Overkick (N=150)		4	3:15		4	2:40
	1700	10	0:55	1500	10	1:00	50 Double Turn 50's Mix Strokes	1200	8	1:15	1100	10	1:20
		5	1:20		3	1:30	100 Smooth		2	1:45		2	2:00
		4	1:15		4	1:25	75 Back (B&N=50)		5	1:10		3	1:15
		2	4:00		2	4:25	300 Descend (B&N=250)		2	4:30		2	5:00
	1700	2	2:05	1500	2	2:15	150 sub 1:35 (1:45, 2:05, 2:23)	1250	2	2:45	1150	2	3:10
		4	2:40		3	2:55	200 Cruise (N=150)		3	3:35		3	3:00
		8	0:50		8	0:55	50 25NotFree/25S		4	1:05		4	1:15
	1700	4	1:35	1500	4	1:45	125 Strong, Last 2:Sub 1:20 (1:28, 1:47, 2:00)	1300	4	2:05	1150	4	2:25
		5	1:30		5	1:35	100 IM		4	2:00		4	2:15
	1700	4	300	1600	4	275	3:45 moderate or descend	1300	4	225	1200	4	200
		5	0:40		4	0:45	50 focus on overkick (BUILD THE SET)		4	0:50		4	1:00
		4	1:20		4	1:25	100 focus on arm speed		3	1:45		2	2:00
		2	2:30		2	2:45	200 minimize stroke count per 25		2	3:20		2	4:00
		4	1:20		4	1:25	100 focus on arm sped		3	1:45		2	2:00
	1700	5	0:40	1600	4	0:45	50 focus overkick	1350	3	0:50	1150	3	1:00
		1	5:15		1	5:45	400 Neg Split (N=250)		1	7:00		1	5:15
		3	2:00		3	2:10	150 Cruise (N=100)		2	2:40		3	2:00
		3	1:55		3	2:05	150 sub1:40 (1:50, 2:13) (N=100 sub1:40)		2	2:35		3	1:55
	1750	6	1:15	1600	4	1:25	75 Bk EZ (N=50)	1300	4	1:40	1150	6	1:15
		5	0:35		5	0:38	50		5	0:45		3	0:55
		5	1:20		4	1:25	100		4	1:55		4	2:00
	1750	5	2:40	1650	5	2:50	200 Just make it	1250	3	3:30	1150	3	4:00

Set Type	Gold Set Dist	Gold Repeats	Gold Interval	Silver Set Dist	Silver Repeats	Silver Interval	SET	Bronze Set Dist	Bronze Repeats	Bronze Interval	Novice Set Dist	Novice Repeats	Novice Interval
General	1750	6	1:05	1650	6	1:10	75 Cruise	1400	4	1:25	1150	6	1:40
		2	5:15		2	5:45	400 1: Strong 2: aim 4:25 (4:52, 5:52)		2	7:00		1	8:00
		5	1:30		4	1:40	100 Back build 2nd 50		3	2:00		3	2:15
	1800	3x		1650	3x			1300	2x		1200	2x	
		{1	2:40		{1	2:55	{200 @2:32 (2:47, 3:22, 3:48)		{1	3:30		{1	4:00
		{2	1:20		{2	1:25	{100 @1:09 (1:16, 1:31, 1:44)		{2	1:45		{2	2:00
		{4	0:45		{3	0:50	{50 @0:31 (0:34, 0:41, 0:47)		{5	1:00		{4	1:05
	1800	2x		1650	2x			1350	1x		1200	1x	
		{1	4:00		{1	4:25	{300 P		{1	5:20		{1	6:00
		{2	2:00		{2	2:10	{150 100IM/50S		{4	2:40		{3	3:00
		{4	1:05		{3	1:10	{75 25K/50 Pace		{6	1:25		{6	1:40
	1800	3	3:50	1700	3	4:10	300 Ascend each swim of set	1300	2	5:05	1200	2	5:45
		3	2:40		2	2:55	200 but you need to make the set		2	3:35		2	4:00
		3	1:30		3	1:40	100		3	2:00		2	2:15
	1850	8	1:35	1600	6	1:45	125 Last 4:Descend	1350	4	2:05	1250	4	2:20
		10	0:30		10	0:35	25 o:Kick on back e:Not Free		10	0:40		6	0:45
		3	2:35		3	2:50	200 1:Cruise 2-3:ALL OUT		3	3:25		3	3:50
Middle Distance	1450	4	1:30	1350	4	1:35	100 @1:04 (1:10 1:25, 1:36)	1050	3	1:50	1000	3	2:15
		2	6:00		2	6:35	400 Descend (N=300)		2	8:00		2	6:45
		5	0:50		3	0:55	50 GOLF		1	1:05		2	1:15
	1500	5	2:35	1300	4	2:50	200 1-2:last 100 fast 3-5:descend (N=175)	1100	4	3:25	1000	4	3:25
		1	6:25		1	7:00	400 IM (B=200,N=100)		1	4:30		2	2:30
		1	1:20		1	1:30	100 ALL OUT		1	1:50		1	2:00
	1500	2x		1400	2x			1200	2x		1100	2x	
		{1	5:30		{1	6:05	{450 100BLAST/50EZ (B&N=300)		{1	4:55		{1	5:30
		{2	1:30		{2	1:40	{100 IM EZ (C=75 Fly/Bk/Br x25 EZ)		{2	1:30		{1	2:15
		{3	0:55		{2	1:00	{50 Kick Desc1-3		{3	1:20		{3	1:25

20-25 Minutes

Set Type	Gold Dist	Gold Reps	Gold Int	Silver Dist	Silver Reps	Silver Int	SET	Bronze Dist	Bronze Reps	Bronze Int	Novice Dist	Novice Reps	Novice Int
Middle Distance	1550	6	0:45	1300	6	0:50	50 Drill/Build x25	1250	5	0:55	1000	4	1:05
		4	175		4	150	2:25 1-3:Desc, 4:Last 50 Fast		4	150		4	125
		6	0:30		4	0:35	25 EZ/FLOAT		4	0:40		4	0:45
		4	100		4	75	1:15 ALL OUT		4	75		4	50
	1600	6	1:55	1450	5	2:05	150 1-3:Cruise 4-6:@1:40 (1:50, 2:13, 2:30)	1200	4	2:35	1100	4	2:55
		4	1:40		4	1:50	100 Bk (N=50)		3	2:15		4	1:15
		2	1:50		2	2:00	150 @1:40 (1:50, 2:13, 2:30)		2	2:25		2	2:45
	1650	3	2:10	1450	3	2:25	150 Just Make em	1250	3	2:50	1100	2	3:15
		3	0:25		3	0:30	25		3	0:30		2	0:40
		3	1:40		3	1:50	125		3	2:10		2	2:30
		3	0:45		3	0:50	50		3	1:00		2	1:05
		3	1:20		3	1:25	100		1	1:45		2	2:00
		3	1:05		1	1:10	100		1	1:25		2	1:40
	1650	10	1:30	1450	8	1:40	100 Sub 1:00 (1:06, 1:20, 1:30)	1250	6	2:00	1150	6	2:15
		1	2:00		1	2:10	150 50Bk/50Swim/50Br		1	2:40		1	2:30
		1	6:15		1	6:45	500 Cruise (N=400)		1	8:20		1	7:30
	1700	6	1:20	1500	5	1:30	100 @ 1:07 (1:14, 1:29, 1:41)	1300	5	1:45	1200	5	2:00
		3	2:35		3	2:50	200 neg split (N=150)		2	3:25		2	2:55
		5	1:20		4	1:30	100 Cruise		4	1:45		4	2:00
	1700	4	0:45	1500	4	0:50	50 Descend to 32 (35, 43, 48)	1300	4	1:00	1150	3	1:05
		4	1:12		3	1:20	100		3	1:35		2	1:50
		2	2:45		2	3:00	200 Pull		2	3:40		2	4:10
		4	1:20		3	1:30	100 Overkick		2	1:45		2	2:00
		4	0:45		4	0:50	50 Descend to 30 (33, 40, 45)		4	1:00		4	1:05
		2	1:00		2	1:05	50 Kick		–	–		–	–

Set Type	Set Dist (Gold)	Repeats (Gold)	Interval (Gold)	Set Dist (Silver)	Repeats (Silver)	Interval (Silver)	SET	Set Dist (Bronze)	Repeats (Bronze)	Interval (Bronze)	Set Dist (Novice)	Repeats (Novice)	Interval (Novice)
Middle Distance	1700	4	1:55	1550	4	2:05	150	1300	3	2:30	1100	3	2:55
		8	0:40		5	0:45	50		5	0:50		5	1:00
		7	1:17		7	1:25	100		6	1:42		4	1:55
	1700	3	0:55	1550	3	1:05	75 (B&N=50) {JUST	1300	3	0:50	1100	3	0:55
		2	0:50		2	1:00	75 (B&N=50) {MAKE		2	0:45		2	0:50
		1	0:45		1	0:55	75 (B&N=50) {IT!		1	0:40		1	0:45
		1	2:00		1	2:15	100 Bk EZ		1	2:40		2	2:50
		3	1:55		2	2:10	150 (B=100) build last 50		2	1:45		-	-
		1	2:00		1	2:15	100 Bk EZ		1	2:40		-	-
		1	7:15		1	8:00	600 Sprint Pyramid (25Fast/25EZ/50Fast/50EZ/75Fast/75EZ/75Fast/75EZ/50Fast/50EZ/25Fast/25EZ)		1	9:40		1	10:50
	1750	3	2:00	1500	3	2:10	150 Steady	1200	2	2:40	1100	2	3:00
		4	1:55		3	2:05	150 sub1:40 (1:50, 2:13, 2:30)		2	2:35		2	2:50
		3	1:30		3	1:40	100 IM		3	2:00		2	2:15
		1	3:45		1	4:05	300 FAST		1	5:00		1	5:30
	1750	2	300	1600	2	275	3:50 #1:Moderate #2:Strong	1250	2	225	1050	2	200
		4	1:20		4	1:25	100 Moderate		-	-		-	-
		3	1:15		3	1:20	100 Strong (N=75)		3	1:45		3	1:30
		2	1:10		2	1:15	100 Fast (N=75)		2	1:40		2	1:25
		1	1:05		1	1:10	100 ALL OUT (N=75)		1	1:30		1	1:15
		3	0:50		1	1:05	50 EZ Not Free		4	1:15		4	1:25
	1800	3x {3	1:20	1500	3x {3	1:30	{100 Cruise	1200	2x {3	1:45	1200	2x {3	1:55
		{2	1:15		{2	1:25	{100 Just Make It		{2	1:40		{2	1:50
		{1	1:10		{2	1:20	{100 Fast		{1	1:35		{1	1:45

Set Type	| Gold — Repeats	Interval	Set Dist	| Silver — Repeats	Interval	Set Dist	SET	| Bronze — Repeats	Interval	Set Dist	| Novice — Repeats	Interval	Set Dist
Middle Distance	2	0:35		2	0:40		50 Just Make it	2	0:45		2	0:55	
	2	2:25		2	2:40		200 ‖	2	3:10		2	3:40	
	1	5:10		1	5:40		400 ‖	1	6:50		1	7:15	
	1	4:50	1800	1	5:30	1600	400 ‖	–	–	1350	–	–	1200
	2	2:20		1	2:35		200 ‖	2	3:05		1	3:30	
	2	0:32		2	0:35		50 V	1	0:45		2	0:50	
	5x			4x				3x			3x		
	{1	1:20		{1	1:30		{100	{1	1:45		{1	2:00	
	{1	1:15	1800	{1	1:25	1650	{100	{1	1:40	1350	{1	1:55	1200
	{1	1:10		{1	1:20		{100	{1	1:35		{1	1:50	
	4	1:00		6	1:05		75 last 25 sprint	6	1:20		4	1:30	
	1	5:50		1	6:15		500 (aim for 15 sec rest)	1	7:45		–	–	
	1	1:20		1	1:25		100 ‖	1	1:45		1	2:00	
	1	4:45		1	5:05		400 ‖	1	6:15		1	7:15	
	1	2:30	1850	1	2:40	1750	200 ‖	1	3:15	1450	1	3:45	1250
	1	3:35		1	3:50		300 V	–	–		1	5:30	
	1	1:00		1	1:05		50 EZ	1	1:10		1	1:30	
	3	1:25		2	1:30		100 3strokes sprint / 3 strokes EZ	2	1:55		2	2:00	
	2	3:00		2	3:20		250 Neg Split	2	4:00		2	4:30	
	2	1:30		2	1:40		100 IM	2	2:00		1	2:15	
	3	0:45	1900	2	0:50	1750	50 25 Swim / 25 Heads Up Free	1	1:00	1450	2	1:10	1300
	3	1:30		2	1:40		100 IM	2	2:00		1	2:15	
	3	3:00		3	3:20		250 Descend	2	4:00		2	4:30	

31

Set Type	Gold Set Dist	Gold Repeats	Gold Interval	Silver Set Dist	Silver Repeats	Silver Interval	SET	Bronze Set Dist	Bronze Repeats	Bronze Interval	Novice Set Dist	Novice Repeats	Novice Interval
Middle Distance	2000	1	1:25	1800	1	1:30	100 (aim for 20 sec rest)	1600	1	1:45	1300	1	2:05
		1	2:30		1	2:40	200 =		1	3:10		1	3:45
		1	3:35		1	3:50	300 =		1	4:35		1	5:25
		1	4:40		1	5:00	400 =		1	6:00		-	-
		1	3:35		1	3:50	300 =		1	4:35		1	5:25
		1	2:30		1	2:40	200 =		1	3:10		1	3:45
		1	1:25		1	1:30	100 >		1	1:45		2	2:05
		1	5:00		1	3:20	400 (B=200) Ascend by 100		-	-		-	-
	1100	8	1:15	1050	7	1:20	50 25 Under, 25 Sprint w/ driving legs	850	5	1:40	750	5	1:50
		1	2:00		1	2:10	100 EZ		1	2:40		1	3:00
		6	2:00		6	2:10	100 ALL OUT, @50&75 rest for 5 sec, Choice		5	2:40		4	3:00
Speed	1350	3x		1200	2x		Round 1&3: Free | Round 2: Not Free	1100	2x		900	2x	
		{1	1:00		{1	1:05	{50 Dive TIMED		{1	1:20		{1	1:30
		{4	0:35		{6	0:40	{25 BALLS OUT		{5	0:45		{4	0:50
		{3	1:25		{4	1:35	{100 EZ (B&N=75)		{5	1:20		{4	1:35
	1350	4	1:45	1200	3	1:55	100 5strokes hard / 5strokes EZ	1050	3	2:20	950	3	2:40
		1	1:10		1	1:15	75 Steady		1	1:30		1	1:40
		4	1:30		4	1:40	75 FAST		3	2:00		2	2:15
		1	1:10		1	1:15	75 Steady		1	1:30		1	1:40
		5	1:00		4	1:10	50 BLAST		3	1:20		3	1:30
		1	1:10		1	1:15	75 Steady		1	1:30		1	1:40
		7	0:30		4	0:35	25 ALL OUT		3	0:40		2	0:45
		-	-		1	1:15	75 Steady		1	1:30		1	1:40
	1500	16	0:45	1350	13	0:50	50 odds:SPRINT evens:Cruise	1150	9	1:00	1000	7	1:10
		1	2:35		1	3:00	200 Pull (N=150)		1	3:25		1	3:00
		4	1:35		4	1:40	125 Descend (last 25 SPRINT)		4	2:05		4	2:25

Type	Set Dist (Gold)	Repeats (Gold)	Interval (Gold)	Set Dist (Silver)	Repeats (Silver)	Interval (Silver)	SET	Set Dist (Bronze)	Repeats (Bronze)	Interval (Bronze)	Set Dist (Novice)	Repeats (Novice)	Interval (Novice)
Speed	1500	3x {1	2:40	1450	3x {1	2:55	{200 Build (N=150)	1200	2x {1	3:30	1100	2x {1	3:00
		{2	1:20		{2	1:25	{100 Pull		{3	1:45		{3	1:55
		{4	0:40		{4	0:40	{25 BLAST		{4	0:50		{4	0:50
	1550	4	2:00	1350	4	2:15	150 Descend, #1 is Strong	1200	3	2:40	1050	2	3:00
		6	0:55		4	1:00	75 Build 1st&Last 25		5	1:10		5	1:20
		20	0:30		18	0:35	25 (3 Fast/1 EZ/1 One Breath)		15	0:40		15	0:45
	1650	6	1:17	1500	5	1:25	100 Strong	1100	3	1:43	1050	3	1:55
		6	0:37		5	0:40	50		3	0:49		4	0:55
		4	1:20		4	1:30	75 Back EZ (N=50)		4	1:45		4	1:30
		8	0:18		8	0:20	25 Fast Interval		6	0:24		6	0:27
		2	1:00		2	1:05	50 Back EZ		2	1:20		2	1:30
		6	0:17		6	0:19	25 Just Make It		4	0:23		4	0:25
	1700	3	2:40	1500	2	2:55	200 Cruise (N=150)	1300	2	3:25	1100	2	3:30
		4	1:15		4	1:20	100 @1:06 (1:13, 1:28, 1:39)		3	1:40		3	1:55
		R	0:30		R	0:30	R0:30		R	0:30		R	0:30
		3	1:20		3	1:30	100 Bk (N=75)		2	1:45		2	1:30
		5	0:39		5	0:43	50 @31 (34, 41, 47)		5	0:50		5	1:00
		R	0:30		R	0:30	R0:30		R	0:30		R	0:30
		2	1:30		2	1:40	75 BLAST (N=50)		2	2:00		2	1:30
Short Rest Interval	1550	3	0:40	1450	3	0:45	50	1200	3	0:50	1050	3	1:00
		2	0:35		2	0:40	50		2	0:45		2	0:55
		1	0:30		1	0:35	50		1	0:40		1	0:50
		6	0:50		5	0:55	50 25Choice/25Free		6	1:05		3	1:15
		4	1:10		3	1:15	50 Kick		2	1:30		2	1:40
		6	1:35		6	1:45	125 of 50 Build / 50Strong / Rest:05 / 25Sprint		4	2:05		4	2:20

20-25 Minutes

33

Set Type	Gold Dist	Gold Repeats	Gold Interval	Silver Dist	Silver Repeats	Silver Interval	SET	Bronze Dist	Bronze Repeats	Bronze Interval	Novice Dist	Novice Repeats	Novice Interval
Short Rest Interval	1600	4x {6	0:35	1400	4x {5	0:40	{50 Fast (Short Rest)	1200	3x {6	0:45	1050	3x {5	0:55
		{1	2:00		{1	2:10	{100 Bk/Br x50		{1	2:40		{1	3:00
	1600	10	0:50	1500	10	0:55	50 Build/Cruise x25 (choice of equipment)	1250	5	1:05	1050	5	1:15
		8	0:25		4	0:25	25 Not Free Build (mix strokes)		4	0:35		4	0:40
		9	1:15		9	1:20	100 Descend by 3's, Last 1 from a Dive		9	1:40		7	2:00
	1800	3x {3	0:34	1650	3x {3	0:38	{50 Strong (touch & go)	1400	2x {5	0:45	1200	2x {4	0:55
		{1	2:30		{1	2:45	{200 Steady		{1	3:15		{1	3:40
		{3	0:45		{2	0:50	{50 IM Rotation		{3	0:55		{2	1:00
		{1	1:30		{1	1:40	{100 Fast		{1	2:00		{1	2:15
	1800	4	1:45	1750	4	1:55	150 Fast	1500	4	2:15	1250	3	2:35
		4	1:15		4	1:20	100 Mod		4	1:35		3	1:50
		4	0:50		4	0:50	50 EZ		4	0:55		3	1:05
		2	1:15		2	1:20	100		1	1:35		1	1:50
		2	1:45		2	1:55	150 Fast		1	2:15		1	2:35
		4	0:45		2	0:50	25 odds: EZ not free evens:Blast choice		2	1:00		4	1:00
	1850	6	1:00	1700	4	1:05	75 Cruise	1400	4	1:20	1200	4	1:40
		8	0:40		8	0:45	50 1-3,5-7@30 (33, 40, 45); 4&8@35 (39,47,53)		4	0:50		4	1:00
		6	1:15		6	1:25	100 Just Make it!		5	1:40		3	1:55
		8	0:40		8	0:45	50 1-3,5-7@30 (33, 40, 45); 4&8@35 (39,47,53)		8	0:50		8	1:00

34

Set Type	SET	Gold Set Dist	Gold Repeats	Gold Interval	Silver Set Dist	Silver Repeats	Silver Interval	Bronze Set Dist	Bronze Repeats	Bronze Interval	Novice Set Dist	Novice Repeats	Novice Interval
Short Rest Interval	125 1-3:Last 25 Fast ; 4-6:Descend	1850	6	1:30	1750	6	1:40	1450	6	2:00	1300	6	2:15
	25 Kick		8	0:35		4	0:40		4	0:45		2	0:50
	75 Steady		4	1:00		4	1:05		-	-		-	-
	75 Moderate		3	0:55		3	1:00		3	1:15		3	1:25
	75 Strong		2	0:50		2	0:55		2	1:10		2	1:20
	75 Fast		1	0:45		1	0:50		1	1:05		1	1:15
	50 ALLOUT		3	0:40		3	0:45		3	0:50		1	0:55
	50 odds:Fly/Fr evens: Br/Fr	1900	10	1:00	1700	10	1:05	1400	8	1:20	1200	8	1:30
	200 Negative Split		7	2:15		6	2:30		5	3:00		4	3:30
	75 IM Order x75	1200	8	1:20	1100	8	1:30	950	6	1:35	850	6	2:00
	100 25S/75K every 3rd not free		6	1:45		5	1:55		5	2:20		4	2:30
Stroke	100 Desc, Not Free	1250	4	1:50	1100	4	2:00	900	3	2:25	800	3	2:45
	50 Perfect Stroke, Not Free		8	0:55		8	1:00		6	1:15		6	1:25
	25 Sprint every 3rd, Not Free		18	0:25		12	0:30		12	0:35		8	0:40
	150 Fly/Bk/Br x25	1300	6	2:25	1200	6	2:35	1000	5	3:10	850	4	3:25
	50 Kick BLAST		8	0:45		6	0:50		5	1:00		5	1:10
	100 IM	1450	10	1:20	1350	9	1:25	1100	7	1:45	900	5	2:00
	50 Bk		4	0:55		4	1:00		4	1:10		4	1:25
	50 25 Underwater ; 25 Not Free Strong		5	1:00		5	1:05		4	1:20		4	1:30
	25 Fly, 7m Kick Underwater	1500	4	0:25	1300	4	0:30	1100	4	0:35	1050	4	0:35
	50 Breast, Double Pull Outs		3	0:50		3	0:55		3	1:05		3	1:15
	75 Back, 7m Kick Underwater		2	1:10		2	1:20		2	1:35		2	1:45
	25 o: Easy e: Sprint Not Free		8	0:25		6	0:30		4	0:35		4	0:35
	150 K/Dr/Swimx50 strong stroke		3	2:40		2	3:00		1	3:30		1	4:00
	25 o: Easy e: Sprint Free		6	0:25		6	0:30		6	0:35		4	0:35
	75 Fly/Bk/Brx25		4	1:10		4	1:20		4	1:35		4	1:45

Set Type	SET	Gold			Silver			Bronze			Novice		
		Set Dist	Repeats	Interval	Set Dist	Repeats	Interval	Set Dist	Repeats	Interval	Set Dist	Repeats	Interval
Stroke	50 Kick-Drill x25, IM order	1600	8	1:00	1400	8	1:05	1150	7	1:20	1000	8	1:30
	200 IM		6	2:50		5	3:15		4	3:45		3	4:20
	100 IM	1600	1	1:30	1500	1	1:30	1200	1	1:55	1000	1	2:15
	200 IM		1	2:50		1	3:00		1	3:50		1	4:30
	300 reverse IM		1	4:10		1	4:30		1	5:45		1	6:45
	400 IM		1	5:30		1	6:00		-	-		-	-
	300 reverse IM		1	4:10		1	4:30		1	5:45		-	-
	200 IM		1	2:50		1	3:00		1	3:50		1	4:30
	100 IM		1	1:30		-	-		1	1:55		2	2:15
	100 Backstroke	1700	5	1:30	1500	6	1:40	1300	4	1:55	1100	5	2:15
	300 (S&B=225, N=150) 50BC5 / 25 Breast		4	4:20		4	3:35		4	4:20		4	3:15
	200 #1:Bk #2:Bk/IM #3:50Bk/100IM/50Bk #4:IM/Bk #5:IM	1700	5	2:50	1500	4	3:10	1300	3	3:45	1200	3	4:05
	100 o:RevIM e:IM		4	1:30		4	1:40		4	2:00		3	2:15
	75 #1:Fly/Bk/Br #2:Bk/Br/Fr #3:Br/Fr/Fly #4:Fr/Fly/Bk		4	1:00		4	1:10		4	1:20		4	1:30
	150 strong IM	1700	8	2:15	1550	7	2:30	1300	6	3:00	1150	5	3:25
	100 Pull BC5		5	1:20		5	1:25		4	1:45		4	2:00
	{200 Reverse IM (N=100)	1700	3x {1	2:45	1600	3x {1	3:00	1200	2x {1	3:40	1050	2x {1	2:10
	{100 IM		{1	1:30		{1	1:35		{1	2:05		{1	2:20
	{50 IM rotation		{4	0:45		{4	0:50		{4	1:00		{4	1:10
	100 Choice Timed (N=50)		2	2:00		1	2:00		2	2:30		5	1:30
	250 Descend to ALL OUT	1700	4	3:15	1600	4	3:35	1400	4	4:20	1150	3	4:55
	25 4:Br 4:Bk 4:Fly (S,B&N=3,3,3)		12	0:30		8	0:35		8	0:40		8	0:45
	50 1-4:Fly/Bk 5-8:Bk/Br (B&N=1-2, 3-4)		8	0:50		8	0:55		4	1:05		4	1:15

Set Type	Gold Set Dist	Gold Repeats	Gold Interval	Silver Set Dist	Silver Repeats	Silver Interval	SET	Bronze Set Dist	Bronze Repeats	Bronze Interval	Novice Set Dist	Novice Repeats	Novice Interval
Distance	2000	20	0:40	1800	16	0:45	50 Strong	1550	11	0:50	1350	12	1:00
		1	12:10		1	13:20	1000 cruise (N=750)		1	16:10		1	13:40
	2000	2	1000	1850	2	925	12:45 Continuous Swim Variable Speed Tempo 25-50-75-100-125-125-100-75-50-25 w/ 25 sprint btwn each effort	1500	2	750	1350	2	675
	2100	12	0:40	1900	8	0:45	50 sub 0:34 (37, 45, 51)	1650	3	0:55	1400	4	1:00
		2	4:00		2	4:25	300 sub 3:15 (3:34, 4:20, 4:52)		2	5:20		2	6:00
		1	8:15		1	9:05	600 sub 7:00 (7:42, 9:20, 10:30)		1	11:00		1	12:20
		3	1:20		3	1:30	100 descend		3	1:45		-	-
	2100	5	1:20	1900	4	1:30	100 sub 1:05 (1:12, 1:27, 1:38)	1550	3	1:45	1450	3	2:00
		1	1000		1	900	13:20 Pull 50 Pace, 25 Fast		1	750		1	700
		3	1:50		3	2:00	100 K (N=75K)		2	2:25		2	2:00
		1	2:00		1	2:10	100 EZ		1	2:40		1	2:45
		1	2:45		1	3:00	200 TIMED		1	3:40		1	4:00
	2300	6	0:40	2050	1	0:45	50 Pace	1700	2	0:55	1500	6	1:00
		5	5:10		5	5:45	400 #2 & #4, stop at each 100 for 5 sec		4	6:50		3	7:45
	2350	6	0:45	2100	5	0:50	50 Drill/Build	1750	4	1:00	1500	3	1:10
		1	1:00		1	1:20	50 Bk		1	1:30		1	1:30
		2	1000		2	900	13:00 400EZ/300mod/200hard/100Hammer		2	750		2	650
General	1200	12	0:35	1050	11	0:40	25 Dolphin Kick, No Board	900	9	0:45	850	9	0:50
		12	0:35		11	0:40	25 Flutter Kick, No Board		9	0:45		9	0:50
		12	0:40		11	0:45	25 Breaststroke Kick, No Board		9	0:50		8	0:55
		12	0:30		9	0:35	25 Choice Kick BLAST		9	0:40		8	0:45

Set Type	SET	Gold Dist	Gold Reps	Gold Int	Silver Dist	Silver Reps	Silver Int	Bronze Dist	Bronze Reps	Bronze Int	Novice Dist	Novice Reps	Novice Int
General	Deep End												
	{0:45 Vertical Kick arms in streamline position		6x {1	0:45		6x {1	0:45		6x {1	0:45		6x {1	0:45
	{r:15 Treading Water		{r	0:15		{r	0:15		{r	0:15		{r	0:15
	300 (N=200) Drill/Swim x50		1	4:00		1	4:25		1	5:20		1	4:00
	550 300 build/last 250 FAST (Driving legs)		1	6:55		1	7:30		1	9:05		1	10:30
	100 Not Free (Kick focus)	1350	5	1:45	1250	4	1:55	1050	2	2:20	950	2	2:35
	75 ALL OUT Fly/Bk/Brz25		4	1:50		4	2:00		2	2:25		2	2:45
	100 EZ		3	1:30		3	1:40		3	2:00		3	2:15
	150 Strong, LAST 2:Blast		5	1:55		4	2:05		4	2:35		3	2:50
	R0:30		R	0:30		R	0:30		R	0:30		R	0:30
	50 ALL OUT	1550	4	1:00	1400	4	1:05	1200	3	1:20	1050	3	1:30
	200 kick hard aim for 30 sec rest min		4	4:50		4	5:15		3	6:25		3	7:15
	200 pull hard aim for 30 sec rest min	1600	4	2:45	1400	3	3:00	1200	3	3:40	1000	2	4:05
	50 Descend Stroke Count		6	0:40		6	0:45		6	0:50		5	1:00
	350 Moderate		1	4:45		1	5:15		1	6:15		1	7:00
	100 1-3:Descend, 4-5:2nd 25 Build, 6-8:Descend		8	1:20		7	1:30		5	1:45		5	2:00
	25 IM order	1650	8	0:35	1550	8	0:40	1350	8	0:45	1200	4	0:50
	{75 Back (B&N=50)		2x {6	1:15		2x {6	1:20		2x {6	1:05		2x {6	1:15
	{50 Drill	1700	{8	0:50	1600	{7	0:55	1300	{7	1:05	1100	{5	1:15
	25 Kick		10	0:35		10	0:35		10	0:45		10	0:50
	300 Pull 1st 100 is 25Scull/25Build/50FAST		2	4:15		2	4:40		2	5:40		2	6:25
	150 Strong IM (50's of 2 best strokes)	1750	6	2:15	1600	5	2:30	1300	3	3:00	1150	2	3:25
	{300 IM (N=200 IM)		3x {1	4:15		3x {1	4:45		2x {1	5:30		2x {1	4:30
	{100 Best Average	1800	{3	1:25	1500	{2	1:35	1400	{4	1:50	1200	{4	2:05

Column groups: Gold / Silver (left header "Set Dist | Repeats | Interval"); SET (center); Bronze / Novice (right header "Set Dist | Repeats | Interval")

Set Type		Set Dist | Repeats | Interval — Gold	Set Dist | Repeats | Interval — Silver	SET	Set Dist | Repeats | Interval — Bronze	Set Dist | Repeats | Interval — Novice
General	Total	1800	1650	3x	1350	1200
		3x	3x	{5:20 Pull BC5	3x	3x
		{1 400	{1 350	{3:50 Kick	{1 300	{1 250
		{1 200	{1 200		{1 150	{1 150
	Total	1800	1650		1400	1200
		3x	3x	{200 Cruise	2x	2x
		{1 2:40	{1 3:00	{100 See Below	{1 3:30	{1 4:00
		{2 ==>	{2 ==>	{rd1: Pull strong	{3 ==>	{2 ==>
		1:25	1:30	{rd2: Kick strong	1:50	2:10
		1:55	2:05	{rd3: Perfect stroke	2:30	2:45
		1:25	1:30	{50 Strong	-	-
		{4 0:45	{3 0:45		{4 0:55	{4 1:05
	Total	1800	1700		1400	1200
		3 4:00	3 4:20	300 w/Paddles #1:FAST #2:Pull #3: Swim	3 5:20	2 6:00
		3 2:40	3 2:55	200 w/Paddles #1:FAST #2:Pull #3: Swim	2 3:30	2 4:00
		3 2:00	2 2:10	100 Bk Descend	1 2:40	2 3:00
	Total	1800	1700		1400	1200
		3x	3x		2x	2x
		{1 4:00	{1 4:25	{300 Pull DPS (B=350)	{1 6:20	{1 6:00
		{1 2:00	{1 2:10	{100 Kick	{1 2:40	{1 3:00
		{1 2:30	{1 2:00	{200 (S=150) Tempo	{1 3:20	{1 3:45
	Total	1850	1700		1450	1250
		9 0:45	6 0:50	50 Drill/Build	3 1:00	3 1:10
		2 2:30	2 2:45	200 Swim w/ Paddles	2 3:20	2 3:45
		2 2:40	2 2:55	200 Cruise	2 3:35	1 4:00
		2 2:50	2 3:05	200 Sprint last 100	2 3:50	2 4:15
		8 0:30	8 0:35	25 IM order Sprint	4 0:40	4 0:45
	Total	1900	1650		1400	1250
		8 1:00	7 1:05	50 kick Build	6 1:20	5 1:30
		4 1:25	4 1:35	75 Kick Last 25 Fast	4 1:55	4 2:00
		9 1:20	8 1:30	100 Pull w/ Paddles	6 1:45	6 2:00
		12 0:20	8 0:25	25 Breast or Fly / Free x25	8 0:27	4 0:30

Set Type	Gold Dist	Gold Repeats	Gold Interval	Silver Dist	Silver Repeats	Silver Interval	SET	Bronze Dist	Bronze Repeats	Bronze Interval	Novice Dist	Novice Repeats	Novice Interval
General	1900	4	2:35	1700	4	2:50	200 rotate 50 fly through	1400	4	3:25	1250	4	4:00
		2	1:00		2	1:05	50 BK		2	1:20		1	1:30
		10	1:20		8	1:30	100 o:IM e:Free		5	1:45		4	2:00
	1900	1	1000	1700	1	900	12:45 negative split	1350	1	750	1250	1	650
		2	3:55		2	4:20	300 Pull smooth		1	5:15		1	6:00
		3	2:00		2	2:15	100 Kick w/board		3	2:30		3	2:45
	1900	10	0:45	1750	9	0:50	50 hold:35 (38, 46)	1450	7	1:00	1250	5	1:10
		10	1:25		9	1:30	100 sub 1:10 (1:17, 1:33)		7	1:50		6	2:10
		1	5:25		1	5:55	400 @1:14 (1:21, 1:38)		1	7:10		1	8:15
	1900	5	1:25	1750	5	1:35	100 IM FAST	1500	3	1:55	1300	2	2:15
		3	2:35		3	2:50	200 Pull (last 50 build)		3	3:25		3	4:00
		1	7:15		1	7:55	500 75S/25K (N=400)		1	9:40		1	8:45
	1900	6	0:55	1750	3	1:00	50 Under/Over	1400	2	1:15	1350	2	1:20
		12	0:50		9	0:55	50 Double Turn		7	1:05		6	1:15
		1	5:45		1	6:20	300 Breast (double pull out every 3rd turn)		1	7:30		1	8:00
		8	1:45		8	1:55	125 100Build/r:05/25Sprint		6	2:20		6	2:25
	1950	3	2:50	1800	3	3:05	200 Pull	1450	3	3:45	1250	2	4:15
		6	1:00		6	1:05	75 Cruise		4	1:20		4	1:30
		4	1:15		3	1:25	100 Descend		2	1:40		2	2:00
		6	0:55		5	1:00	50 o:Fly e:Bk		4	1:15		4	1:20
		4	0:45		4	0:50	50 FAST		3	1:00		3	1:15

Set Type	Gold Dist	Gold Repeats	Gold Interval	SET	Silver Dist	Silver Repeats	Silver Interval	Bronze Dist	Bronze Repeats	Bronze Interval	Novice Dist	Novice Repeats	Novice Interval
General	2000	1	2:25	175 Steady	1750	1	2:40	1400	-	-	1300	-	-
		7	0:25	25 Build		7	0:30		6	0:35		6	0:40
		2	2:10	150 Negative Split		2	2:20		1	2:50		1	3:10
		6	0:45	50 Overkick		5	0:55		5	1:05		5	1:10
		3	1:45	125 Last 1 FAST		2	1:55		2	2:20		2	2:35
		5	1:05	75 3strokes hard/3 strokes EZ		4	1:10		4	1:25		4	1:35
		3	1:30	100 50steady/50FAST		3	1:40		3	2:00		2	2:15
	2000	10	0:42	50 desc last 5	1800	10	0:45	1500	8	0:55	1350	9	1:00
		5	2:40	200 desc last 3		4	2:55		4	3:35		3	4:00
		1	6:00	400 IM (B&N=200 done as 100IM's)		1	6:35		1	4:00		1	4:30
		1	1:30	100 ALL OUT		1	1:40		1	2:00		1	2:15
	2000	8	0:45	50 Desc	1850	8	0:50	1500	4	1:00	1400	6	1:05
		2	2:35	200 Swim w/Paddles Strong		2	2:50		2	3:25		2	3:50
		4	1:20	100 FAST w/ fins		4	1:25		4	1:55		4	2:00
		4	0:40	50 Desc		3	0:45		4	0:55		4	1:00
		2	0:50	50 Kick w/ board BUST IT		2	0:55		2	1:05		2	1:15
		5	1:30	100 IM		4	1:40		2	2:00		-	-
	2000	1	5:30	300 Kick (B&N=200)	1850	1	6:00	1650	1	4:50	1450	1	5:30
		1	5:00	400 Pull		1	5:30		1	6:40		1	7:30
		1	4:00	300 Drill (B&N=200)		1	4:20		1	3:40		1	4:00
		1	5:00	400 Pull		1	5:30		1	6:40		1	7:30
		6	1:00	75 @48 (52, 1:04)		4	1:05		2	1:20		2	1:30
		3	1:20	100 @1:08 (1:15, 1:30)		3	1:25		3	1:45		1	2:00

25-30 Minutes

Set Type	Set Dist	Repeats	Interval (Gold)	Set Dist	Repeats	Interval (Silver)	SET	Set Dist	Repeats	Interval (Bronze)	Set Dist	Repeats	Interval (Novice)
General	2000	1	6:40	1900	1	7:20	500 Pull aim for 10s rest	1500	–	–	1300	–	–
		1	1:30		1	1:40	100 IM FAST		1	2:00		–	–
		1	5:20		1	5:50	400 Steady		1	7:00		1	8:00
		1	1:30		1	1:40	100 IM FAST		1	2:00		1	2:15
		1	4:00		1	4:25	300 Faster than 400's pace		1	5:15		1	6:00
		1	1:30		1	1:40	100 IM FAST		1	2:00		1	2:15
		1	2:40		1	2:55	200 Faster than 300's pace		1	3:30		1	4:00
		1	1:30		1	1:40	100 IM FAST		1	2:00		1	2:15
		1	1:20		1	1:30	100 Faster than 200's pace (Strong)		1	1:45		1	2:00
		1	1:30		–	–	100 IM FAST		1	2:00		–	–
	2000	6	3:20	1900	6	3:40	250 Desc,1st&last 25 Stroke (1-3:Pull,4-6:Swim)	1600	5	4:25	1350	4	5:00
		10	0:35		8	0:35	25 Not Free Sprint		6	0:45		8	0:45
		5	0:45		4	0:45	50 GOLF (Time + Strokes) Descend		4	1:00		3	1:10
	2150	12	2:00	1900	10	2:15	150 hold sub 1:40 (1:50, 2:14, 2:30)	1600	9	2:40	1450	8	3:00
		1	1:00		1	1:05	50 EZ		1	1:20		1	1:30
		6	0:45		7	0:50	50 Descend		4	1:00		4	1:00
	2250	4	225	1950	4	200	2:50 1st 25 Not Free / Last 25 Fast Free	1700	4	175	1400	4	150
		3	175		3	150	2:45 Strong IM		3	125		3	100
		1	425		1	375	5:00 Each Swim Gets Faster		1	325		1	275
		1	200		1	175	2:30 | — |		1	150		1	125
		2	100		2	75	1:15 V V		2	75		2	50
	2250	2x		2050	2x		Cruise Set	1650	2x		1500	2x	
		{1	3:45		{1	4:00	{300		{1	5:00		{1	5:40
		{2	2:35		{2	2:45	{200		{1	3:25		{1	3:55
		{3	1:20		{2	1:30	{100		{2	1:45		{2	2:00
		5	0:55		5	1:00	50 Kick		5	1:10		2	1:15

25-30 Minutes

Set Type	Gold Set Dist	Gold Repeats	Gold Interval	Silver Set Dist	Silver Repeats	Silver Interval	SET	Bronze Set Dist	Bronze Repeats	Bronze Interval	Novice Set Dist	Novice Repeats	Novice Interval
Middle Distance	1400	12	1:00	1250	9	1:05	50 Descend by 3's (1:Strong, 2:FAST, 3:BLAST)	1000	8	1:20	900	6	1:30
		1	3:00		1	3:15	200 Build to 100 pace		-	-		-	-
		3	4:00		3	4:20	200 > 75cruise/r:10/50build/r:10/50sprint/r:10/25sprint		3	5:20		3	6:00
	1650	2	2:45	1500	2	3:00	150 Pull (B&N=100)	1200	2	2:25	1100	2	2:45
		2	2:45		2	3:00	150 Overkick (B&N=100)		2	2:25		2	2:45
		5	2:45		4	3:00	150 O: 90% E: EZ middle 50 stroke (N=100)		4	3:40		5	2:45
		1	3:30		1	3:50	300 ALL OUT (B&N=200)		1	3:10		1	3:30
	1700	6	3:00	1550	6	3:15	200 100 EZ/50Build/50Sprint	1350	6	4:00	1150	5	4:30
		10	1:00		7	1:10	50 25under/25Blast		3	1:20		3	1:45
	1800	2	0:45	1600	2	0:50	50 FAST	1400	2	1:00	1300	2	1:05
		2	1:30		2	1:40	100 Pick 1 pace		2	2:00		1	2:10
		2	3:00		2	3:20	200 | For		1	4:00		1	4:20
		1	6:00		1	6:40	400 | The		1	8:00		1	8:40
		2	3:00		1	3:20	200 | Whole		1	4:00		1	4:20
		2	1:30		2	1:40	100 V Set		2	2:00		2	2:10
		2	0:45		2	0:50	50 FAST		2	1:00		2	1:05
	1800	16	0:25	1700	16	0:25	25 Spint Drills, Every 4th Sprint	1400	12	0:30	1200	8	0:35
		1	2:00		1	2:00	100 BK EZ		1	2:30		1	3:00
		8	1:45		7	1:50	100 sub1:01 (1:07, 1:20, 1:32)		5	2:20		5	2:40
		1	6:15		1	6:50	500 Long and Strong (N=400)		1	8:20		1	7:30

25-30 Minutes

25-30 Minutes

Set Type	Gold Dist	Gold Repeats	Gold Interval	SET	Silver Dist	Silver Repeats	Silver Interval	Bronze Dist	Bronze Repeats	Bronze Interval	Novice Dist	Novice Repeats	Novice Interval
Middle Distance	1900	3	2:35	200 Desc	1700	2	2:45	1350	2	3:30	1250	2	3:50
		6	0:30	25 Fly		6	0:35		6	0:40		4	0:45
		3	1:55	150 Desc		3	2:05		2	2:35		2	2:55
		6	0:30	25 Bk		6	0:35		6	0:40		6	0:45
		4	1:15	100 Desc		4	1:25		2	1:40		2	2:00
		6	0:30	25 Br		6	0:35		6	0:40		4	0:45
	1950	3	2:40	200 sub 2:10 (2:23, 2:53) (N=150, 2:27)	1750	3	2:55	1500	3	3:20	1300	3	3:00
		3	1:20	100 sub 1:10 (1:17, 1:33, 1:45)		2	1:25		2	1:45		3	2:00
		3	0:40	50 NOT FREE		3	0:45		2	0:55		1	1:00
		3	1:20	100 sub 1:12 (1:19, 1:36, 1:48)		2	1:25		2	1:45		2	2:00
		3	2:40	200 sub 2:14 (2:27, 2:58) (N=150, 2:32)		3	2:55		2	3:20		2	3:00
	1950	1	3:30	250 FAST (N=200)	1850	1	3:50	1500	1	4:20	1350	1	4:15
		5	1:15	100 @1:06 (1:13, 1:29, 1:39)		4	1:25		3	1:40		3	1:50
		R	0:45	R0:45		R	0:45		R	0:45		R	0:45
		1	3:00	200 FAST (N=150)		1	3:20		1	4:00		1	3:20
		4	1:10	100 @1:05 (1:12, 1:27, 1:37)		4	1:18		3	1:35		3	1:45
		R	0:50	R0:50		R	0:50		R	0:50		R	0:50
		1	2:30	150 FAST (N=100)		1	2:45		1	3:20		1	2:30
		6	0:55	75 sub50 (55, 1:06, 1:15)		6	1:00		4	1:15		4	1:20
	2000	1	3:30	250 Loosen (B&N=200)	1750	1	3:50	1500	1	3:45	1300	1	4:15
		2	1:40	125 Cruise (B&N=100)		2	1:50		2	1:50		2	2:00
		2	1:55	125 Blast (B&N=100)		2	2:05		2	2:05		2	2:20
		4	0:55	50 Not Free		4	1:05		3	1:15		3	1:30
		2	2:55	200 sub 2:12 (2:25, 2:56, 3:18) neg split		1	3:15		2	3:55		1	4:15
		4	1:30	125 @1:25 (1:33, 1:58, 2:08)		4	1:40		2	2:00		2	2:15
		6	0:27	25 Not Free		4	0:30		4	0:35		4	0:40

25-30 Minutes

44

Set Type	SET	Gold Set Dist	Gold Repeats	Gold Interval	Silver Set Dist	Silver Repeats	Silver Interval	Bronze Set Dist	Bronze Repeats	Bronze Interval	Novice Set Dist	Novice Repeats	Novice Interval
Middle Distance	400 steady	2000	1	5:20	1800	1	5:50	1500	1	7:05	1300	1	8:00
	300 build each 100		2	4:00		2	4:25		1	5:20		1	6:00
	200 desc		3	2:40		3	2:55		2	3:35		2	4:00
	100 last 2 fast		4	1:20		2	1:30		4	1:45		2	2:00
	2:15 last 2 FAST	2100	4	175	1800	4	150	1500	4	125	1400	4	125
	50 IM order		3	0:50		4	0:55		3	1:05		3	1:15
	4:15 All Out		1	300		1	275		1	225		1	200
	125 last 1 FAST		4	1:35		2	1:45		2	2:05		2	2:20
	50 IM order		3	0:50		4	0:55		3	1:05		2	1:15
	4:15 All Out		1	300		1	275		1	225		1	200
	50 Strong	2100	8	0:40	1850	8	0:45	1550	4	0:55	1350	2	1:00
	100 Cruise		4	1:25		4	1:35		3	1:55		2	2:15
	225 150 BLAST ; 25 Super EZ ; 50 BLAST		2	3:00		2	3:20		2	4:00		2	4:30
	250 Slow		1	4:25		1	4:50		1	5:50		1	6:30
	200 BLAST		1	3:00		1	3:20		1	4:00		1	4:30
	100 Cruise		2	1:25		2	1:35		1	1:55		1	2:15
	50 Strong		4	0:40		4	0:45		1	0:55		1	1:00
	125 Last 2 Fast	2100	6	1:40	1900	5	1:50	1600	4	2:10	1400	4	2:30
	25 o:Kick e:Choice		6	0:35		7	0:40		8	0:40		4	1:00
	8:00 - Broken swims		2x	(600)		2x	(550)		2x	(450)		2x	(400)
	{100		{3	r:05		{3	r:05		{2	r:05		{2	r:05
	{75		{2	r:05		{2	r:05		{2	r:05		{2	r:05
	{50		{3	r:05		{2	r:05		{2	r:05		{1	-

Set Type	Gold Set Dist	Gold Repeats	Gold Interval	Silver Set Dist	Silver Repeats	Silver Interval	SET	Bronze Set Dist	Bronze Repeats	Bronze Interval	Novice Set Dist	Novice Repeats	Novice Interval
Middle Distance	2100	1	2:40	1900	1	2:50	200 EZ	1650	1	3:20	1400	-	-
		2	2:20		2	2:30	175 Descend		2	2:55		2	3:30
		2	2:00		2	2:10	150 | Pace		2	2:30		2	3:00
		2	1:40		2	1:50	125 |		2	2:05		2	2:30
		4	1:20		2	1:25	100 V		2	1:40		2	2:00
		4	1:00		4	1:05	75 Goal mile Pace		2	1:15		2	1:30
		4	0:40		4	0:45	50 Goal 500 Pace		2	0:50		2	1:00
		4	0:20		4	0:25	25 All Out		4	0:25		2	0:30
	2200	3	1:00	1950	3	1:05	75 Maintain Pace	1600	3	1:20	1450	3	1:35
		2	0:55		2	1:00	75 |		2	1:15		2	1:25
		1	0:50		1	0:55	75 V		1	1:10		1	1:15
		3	1:30		2	1:40	100 IM		3	2:00		3	2:15
		4	1:50		3	2:00	150 100Strong/50FAST		2	2:25		2	2:45
		3	0:55		3	1:00	50 EZ Bk		3	1:15		2	1:30
		2	4:00		2	4:25	300 TIMED		1	5:20		1	5:45
		4	0:25		4	0:30	25 IM order		4	0:35		-	-
	2200	3	2:25	2000	3	2:35	200	1700	2	3:10	1500	1	3:35
		1	3:25		1	3:45	200 (B&N=150) Bk		1	3:20		1	3:45
		3	2:25		2	2:35	200		2	3:10		2	3:35
		1	3:25		1	3:45	200 (B&N=150) Bk		1	3:20		1	3:45
		3	2:25		3	2:35	200 Desc		3	3:10		3	3:35
	2200	8	2:35	2000	7	2:50	200 rotate through a 25 Blast	1700	6	3:05	1500	5	3:50
		1	2:00		1	2:10	100 BK/FR/BR/FRx25		1	2:40		1	3:00
		5	1:20		5	1:30	100 Desc		4	1:45		4	1:55

25-30 Minutes

Set Type	Gold Set Dist	Gold Repeats	Gold Interval	Silver Set Dist	Silver Repeats	Silver Interval	SET	Bronze Set Dist	Bronze Repeats	Bronze Interval	Novice Set Dist	Novice Repeats	Novice Interval
Middle Distance	2200	1	0:40	2000	1	0:45	50 Make it by 5 sec	1750	1	0:50	1500	1	1:00
		2	1:20		2	1:30	100	10 sec		2	1:40		2	2:00
		3	2:00		3	2:15	150	20 sec		3	2:30		3	3:00
		4	2:40		3	3:00	200	30 sec		3	3:20		2	4:00
		3	2:00		3	2:15	150	20 sec		2	2:30		2	3:00
		2	1:20		2	1:30	100	10 sec		1	1:40		1	2:00
		1	0:40		1	0:45	50 ∨ 5 sec		1	0:50		–	–
	2250	6	1:10	2050	6	1:15	100 Cruise	1650	4	1:30	1450	4	1:45
		6	2:30		5	2:45	200 Pull (N=150)		4	3:20		4	2:50
		1	6:00		1	6:35	450 50EZ/25SPRINT		1	8:00		1	9:00
	2250	3x		2100	3x			1700	2x		1500	2x	
		{1	0:40		{-	–	{50		{3	0:50		{1	1:00
		{1	1:15		{1	1:20	{100		{1	1:40		{1	1:55
		{1	2:30		{1	2:40	{200		{1	3:20		{1	3:45
		{1	4:55		{1	5:20	{400		{1	6:30		{1	7:30
Speed	1450	6	1:00	1350	4	1:10	50 Kick	1100	4	1:20	1000	4	1:30
		1	3:00		1	3:20	200 Build		1	4:00		1	4:30
		6	1:45		6	1:55	100 FAST		4	2:20		4	2:40
		5	0:50		5	0:55	50 Sprint		4	1:05		3	1:15
		4	0:30		4	0:30	25 All Out		4	0:40		2	0:45
	1500	3x		1350	3x			1050	3x		900	3x	
		{4	0:40		{3	0:45	{50 Build		{3	0:55		{2	1:00
		{8	0:30		{8	0:30	{25 3-Sprint 1-EZ		{6	0:40		{6	0:45
		{2	1:10		{2	1:20	{50 Back EZ		{1	1:35		{1	2:00

Set Type	Gold Set Dist	Gold Repeats	Gold Interval	Silver Set Dist	Silver Repeats	Silver Interval	SET	Bronze Set Dist	Bronze Repeats	Bronze Interval	Novice Set Dist	Novice Repeats	Novice Interval
Speed	1850	4	1:50	1650	3	2:00	150 last 2 sub 1:40 (1:50, 2:13, 2:30)	1400	3	2:25	1250	3	2:45
		4	1:15		4	1:25	75 Not Free		4	1:40		2	1:50
		4	1:15		4	1:20	100 last 3 sub 1:05 (1:12, 1:26, 1:37)		4	1:40		4	1:50
		4	0:55		3	1:00	50 Not Free		2	1:15		2	1:30
		R	0:20		R	0:20	R0:20		R	0:20		R	0:20
		2	1:20		2	1:30	75 FAST		2	1:45		2	2:00
		8	0:25		8	0:30	25 Not Free		-	-		-	-
	1850	9	0:45	1700	9	0:50	50 2:Strong/1:Fast	1400	9	1:00	1300	9	1:05
		4	2:25		4	2:40	175 Cruise		2	3:15		2	3:40
		6	0:45		6	0:50	50 2:Strong/1:Fast		6	1:00		6	1:05
		10	0:35		4	0:40	25 o:Kick e:Not Free		6	0:45		2	0:50
		3	0:45		3	0:50	50 2:Strong/1:Fast		3	1:00		3	1:05
	2000	4x {3	0:45	1800	4x {3	0:50	{50 sub 30 (33, 40, 45)	1500	3x {3	0:55	1350	3x {3	1:05
		{2	1:20		{2	1:25	{100 @1:02 (1:08, 1:22, 1:33)		{2	1:45		{2	2:00
		{1	2:05		{1	1:30	{150 (S&N=100) EZ		{1	2:45		{1	2:05
	2000	3	0:40	1850	3	0:45	50 @ 31 (34, 41, 46)	1500	3	0:55	1300	3	1:00
		2	1:00		2	1:05	75 @ 47 (51, 1:03, 1:11)		2	1:20		2	1:30
		1	1:20		1	1:30	100 @1:03 (1:10, 1:24, 1:35)		1	1:50		1	2:00
		2	1:00		2	1:05	75 @47 (51, 1:03, 1:11)		2	1:20		2	1:30
		3	0:40		3	0:45	50 @31 (34, 41, 46)		3	0:55		3	1:00
		8	0:20		8	0:25	25 Blast		8	0:30		8	0:30
		6	0:55		5	1:05	50 Bk		4	1:15		2	1:30
		2	5:00		2	4:10	400 (S&N=300) last 100 IM FAST		1	6:40		1	5:40
SRI	1850	7	2:30	1650	6	2:45	200 last 2 fast	1400	5	3:15	1250	5	3:45
		7	0:55		7	1:00	50 Kick w/ board		6	1:10		3	1:20
		4	0:40		4	0:40	25 Form focus Sprints		4	0:50		4	1:00

Set Type	SET	Gold Set Dist	Gold Repeats	Gold Interval	Silver Set Dist	Silver Repeats	Silver Interval	Bronze Set Dist	Bronze Repeats	Bronze Interval	Novice Set Dist	Novice Repeats	Novice Interval
Short Rest Interval	Interval set is on:	2000	5X	5:20	1750	5X	5:20	1600	4X	6:40	1400	4X	6:40
	{100 r:05		{2	@1:07		{2	@1:13		{2	@1:29		{1	@1:40
	{50 r:05		{2	@0:31		{2	@0:34		{2	@0:41		{2	@0:46
	{25 r:05		{4	@0:14		{2	@0:16		{4	@0:18		{2	@0:21
	100	2150	8	1:15	1950	8	1:20	1600	8	1:40	1450	8	1:55
	50 Not Free		2	1:00		2	1:05		2	1:20		1	2:00
	75		8	0:55		8	1:00		8	1:10		8	1:25
	25 Not Free		2	0:30		2	0:35		-	-		-	-
	200 IM (B=100IM)		3	2:40		2	3:00		1	1:50		-	-
	400 Strong	2200	2	5:05	2000	2	5:35	1700	2	6:50	1500	2	7:40
	100 Faster than 400 Pace		6	1:15		4	1:25		6	1:40		4	1:50
	75 Blast		4	1:00		4	1:05		4	1:20		4	1:30
	500 Pull		1	6:30		1	7:10		-	-		-	-
	{200 strong	2400	4X {1	2:20	2200	4X {1	2:35	1800	3X {1	3:05	1500	3X {1	3:30
	{150 strong		{1	1:45		{1	1:55		{1	2:20		{1	2:40
	{100 Fast		{1	1:10		{1	1:15		{1	1:35		{1	1:45
	{50 easy (N=25)		{3	0:40		{2	0:45		{3	1:00		{2	0:50
Stroke	75 Kick (no flutter)	1600	8	1:30	1450	8	1:40	1200	8	1:50	1050	6	2:15
	25 o:Drill e:Sprint		12	0:30		10	0:30		8	0:40		8	0:45
	100 Back		7	1:40		6	1:50		4	2:15		4	2:30

Set Type	SET	Gold Set Dist	Gold Repeats	Gold Interval	Silver Set Dist	Silver Repeats	Silver Interval	Bronze Set Dist	Bronze Repeats	Bronze Interval	Novice Set Dist	Novice Repeats	Novice Interval
Stroke	2x	1800	2x		1600	2x		1400	2x		1200	2x	
	{75 Cruise Not Free		{4	1:15		{3	1:25		{2	1:40		{2	2:00
	{25 Sprint Not Free		{4	0:35		{3	0:40		{2	0:45		{2	0:50
	{250 EZ (N=225)		{1	3:20		{1	3:40		{1	4:25		{1	4:35
	{75 last 2 FAST Free		{3	1:15		{3	1:25		{3	1:40		{2	1:50
	{25 EZ		{1	0:40		{1	0:45		{1	0:55		{1	1:00
	125 1st & Last 25 IM order	1800	8	1:40	1700	8	1:50	1350	6	2:10	1250	6	2:30
	75 Cruise		4	1:05		4	1:10		4	1:25		4	1:40
	50 Not Free		6	0:55		5	1:00		4	1:15		2	1:30
	50 Build		4	0:45		3	0:50		2	1:00		2	1:05
	2x	1850	2x		1650	2x		1350	2x		1200	2x	
	{125 Rd1:Cruise Rd2:sub1:25 (1:34, 1:54, 2:08)		{4	1:40		{4	1:50		{3	2:15		{3	2:30
	{50 IM rot		{3	0:50		{3	0:55		{3	1:05		{3	1:15
	R0:10 after set		R	0:10		R	0:10		R	0:10		R	0:10
	50 Not Free		5	0:50		3	0:55		3	1:05		-	-
	50 o:EZ e:sub30 (33, 40, 45)		6	0:45		4	0:50		3	1:00		3	1:10
	100 o:IM e:Bk	1850	8	1:30	1700	8	1:40	1350	6	2:00	1200	5	2:15
	100 EZ		1	2:00		1	2:00		1	2:30		1	3:00
	75 Free S/D/Sx25		10	1:10		8	1:15		6	1:35		6	1:45
	50 Race Stroke EZ/Hardx25		4	0:50		4	0:55		4	1:05		3	1:15
	150 100 Not Free (rotate IM strokes) / 50Fr	1900	6	2:15	1800	6	2:30	1500	4	3:00	1250	3	3:30
	25 IM Order Stroke=Sprint Free=EZ		16	0:30		12	0:35		12	0:40		8	0:45
	200 Descend		3	2:25		3	2:40		3	3:10		3	3:45

Set Type	Gold Set Dist	Gold Repeats	Gold Interval	Silver Set Dist	Silver Repeats	Silver Interval	SET	Bronze Set Dist	Bronze Repeats	Bronze Interval	Novice Set Dist	Novice Repeats	Novice Interval
Stroke	1900	1	5:45	1800	1	6:15	400 IM as 4 100 IMs	1500	1	7:30	1300	-	-
		1	4:20		1	4:45	300 IM		1	5:40		1	6:30
		1	2:55		1	3:15	200 IM as 2 100 IMs		1	3:50		1	4:30
		1	1:30		-	-	100 IM		1	2:00		3	2:20
		1	2:55		1	3:15	200 IM		1	3:50		1	4:30
		1	4:20		1	4:45	300 IM as 3 100 IMs		1	5:40		1	6:30
		1	5:45		1	6:15	400 IM		-	-		-	-
	1950	6	1:10	1650	6	1:20	75 1st25 Weak Stroke, last25 Strong Stroke	1500	4	1:35	1200	4	1:55
		5	4:20		4	4:50	300 Mid 100 IM, last 100 faster than first		4	5:45		3	6:45
	2000	5	400	1750	5	350	#1=5:40 IM #2=5:30 300IM/100S #3=5:20 2IM/2S #4=5:10 100IM/300S #5-5:00 400S	1500	5	300	1250	5	250
	2000	10	1:30	1800	9	1:40	100 IM (steady)	1500	7	2:00	1300	6	2:15
		10	1:20		9	1:30	100 2nd 25 not free		8	1:45		7	2:00
	2000	4x		1800	4x			1500	3x		1350	3x	
		{1	1:15		{1	1:20	{100 Free		{1	1:40		{1	1:55
		{1	1:30		{1	1:40	{100 IM		{1	2:00		{1	2:15
		{1	1:20		{1	1:30	{100 Fr/stroke x25		{1	1:50		{1	2:05
		{1	1:30		{1	1:40	{100 revIM		{1	2:00		{1	2:15
		{1	1:30		{1	0:50	{100 stroke (S&N=50)		{1	2:00		{1	1:10
	2000	4	3:00	1800	3	3:15	200 o: rev IM e: IM	1600	2	3:50	1300	2	5:00
		4	4:15		4	4:40	300 (Novice do 2-4)		4	5:30		3	6:30
							{#1 - 300IM , #2 - 100Free/200IM						
							{#3 - 200Free/100IM , #4 - 300Free						
	2100	8	1:30	2000	7	1:35	100 1st 25 Not Free	1600	7	2:00	1300	9	2:15
		3	5:45		3	6:15	400 IM		2	7:40		1	8:40

SET	Gold Rep	Gold Int	Silver Rep	Silver Int	Bronze Rep	Bronze Int	Novice Rep	Novice Int
500 ALL OUT (N=400)	1	6:40	1	7:05	1	8:45	1	8:00
100 Just make it	1	1:30	1	1:35	1	2:00	1	2:15
200 FAST	1	2:40	1	2:50	1	3:30	1	4:00
100 o:Just make it e: BLAST	3	1:30	3	1:35	1	2:00	1	2:15
50 ALL OUT	1	0:40	-	-	-	-	-	-
100 o:Just make it e: BLAST	3	1:30	-	-	-	-	-	-
200 FAST	1	2:40	1	2:50	1	3:30	1	4:00
100 Just make it	1	1:30	3	1:35	1	2:00	1	2:15
500 ALL OUT (N=400)	1	6:40	1	7:05	1	8:45	1	8:00
Set Dist	2250		2100		1700		1500	
100 FAST	6	1:20	6	1:30	4	1:45	2	2:00
50EZ	1	1:00	1	1:00	1	1:15	1	1:30
1000 (B&N = 750) Pull 8x{100FR/25Stroke}	1	13:20	1	14:40	1	13:30	1	15:00
450 (S,B,N=300K) Kick pyramid	1	8:15	1	6:00	1	7:15	1	9:15
100EZ (N=50 EZ)	1	1:45	1	2:00	1	2:15	1	1:45
100 ALL OUT	1	1:30	1	1:40	1	2:00	1	2:15
Set Dist	2300		2150		1700		1450	
50 Drill	8	0:45	5	0:50	6	1:00	4	1:10
550 Hold constant Pace	3	7:20	3	8:00	2	9:45	2	11:00
50 Ascend #1 sub 32 (35, 42)	6	0:50	5	0:55	6	1:05	5	1:15
Set Dist	2350		2150		1700		1550	
10:00 #1-Cruise, #2-Build by 200's	2	800	2	725	2	600	2	525
6:00 FAST & NegSplit	2	400	2	350	2	300	2	275
Set Dist	2400		2150		1800		1600	
Rds 3 & 5 Pull	7X		6x		5x		4x	
300 Cruise	{1	3:45	{1	4:20	{1	5:20	{1	5:35
50 Strong	{1	0:45	{1	0:55	{1	1:00	{2	1:10
Set Dist	2450		2100		1750		1600	

Set Type	Gold	Silver	SET	Bronze	Novice
Distance	1 / 1000	1 / 900	13:00 MAX EFFORT SWIMS (lots of rest)	1 / 750	1 / 675
	1 / 750	1 / 675	9:45	1 / 600	1 / 500
	1 / 500	1 / 450	6:35	1 / 375	1 / 350
	1 / 250	1 / 225	3:15	1 / 175	1 / 175
Set Dist	2500	2250		1900	1700
	2 / 525	2 / 475	6:30 Swim	2 / 400	2 / 350
	1 / 0:50	1 / 0:55	50 Bk	1 / 1:05	1 / 1:30
	1 / 1:20	1 / 1:30	100	1 / 1:40	1 / 1:55
	1 / 1:15	1 / 1:25	100	1 / 1:35	1 / 1:50
	1 / 1:10	1 / 1:20	100	1 / 1:30	1 / 1:45
	2 / 0:50	2 / 0:55	50 Bk	2 / 1:05	1 / 1:30
	4 / 225	4 / 200	2:55 Pull	4 / 175	4 / 150
	3 / 0:50	2 / 0:55	50 Bk	1 / 1:05	- / -
Set Dist	2550	2300		2000	1700
	1 / 12:00	1 / 13:10	1000 @PACES with last 100 ALL OUT	1 / 15:55	- / -
	@1:15	@1:23	(400 @	@1:40	-
	@1:10	@1:17	{300 @	@1:34	-
	@1:05	@1:12	{200 @	@1:27	-
	4 / 0:55	3 / 1:00	50 Bk	3 / 1:15	-
	1 / 7:15	1 / 8:00	600 @PACES	1 / 9:40	2 / 10:55
	@1:15	@1:23	{300 @	@1:40	2 / @1:52
	@1:10	@1:17	{200 @	@1:34	1 / @1:45
	@1:05	@1:12	{100 @	@1:27	1 / @1:38
	4 / 0:55	3 / 1:00	50 Bk	3 / 1:15	2 / 1:25
	1 / 3:30	1 / 4:05	300 @PACES	-	1 / 5:15
	@1:10	@1:17	{200 @	-	2 / @1:45
	@1:05	@1:12	{100 @	-	1 / @1:38
	4 / 0:55	2 / 1:00	50 Bk	-	-
	1 / 1:10	1 / 1:20	100 Max Effort	1 / 1:30	1 / 1:45
Set Dist	2600	2400		2000	1800

30-35 Minutes

Set Type	Gold Dist	Gold Repeats	Gold Interval	Silver Dist	Silver Repeats	Silver Interval	SET	Bronze Dist	Bronze Repeats	Bronze Interval	Novice Dist	Novice Repeats	Novice Interval
Dist	2600	4	375	2400	4	350	5:00 Pull Descend	2000	4	300	1700	4	250
		4	200		4	175	2:30 Swim Descend		4	150		4	125
		4	75		4	75	1:15 Back Descend		4	50		4	50
General	1700	24	0:30	1600	20	0:30	25 Kick/Drill x25 IM order	1300	16	0:40	1200	16	0:45
		1	8:30		1	9:30	600 BC 7-3-5-3 x50		1	11:30		1	12:45
		10	1:00		10	1:05	50 Kick no board		6	1:20		4	1:30
	2000 (4x)	{1	3:00	1900 (4x)	{1	3:20	{200 Drill/Buildx100	1500 (3x)	{1	4:00	1350 (3x)	{1	4:30
		{2	1:30		{2	1:40	{100 Strong, BC 5-7		{2	2:00		{2	2:15
		{4	0:30		{3	0:35	{25 Sprint		{4	0:40		{2	0:45
	2200	6	1:20	2000	4	1:25	100 Dist per Stroke, (Zoomers Optional)	1700	3	1:45	1500	1	2:00
		3	0:50		3	0:55	50 o:Bk e:Fly EZ		2	1:05		2	1:15
		2	5:10		2	5:40	400 (B&N=350) Dist per Stroke		2	5:45		2	6:45
		3	1:00		3	1:05	50 o:Br e:Bk EZ		2	1:20		2	1:15
		4	1:45		4	1:55	125 3rd 25 fly w/ Fins or Zoomers		4	2:20		4	2:35
	2200	1	5:30	2000	1	6:00	400 alternating 100rev IM & 100S	1700	1	7:15	1500	1	8:15
		12	1:30		10	1:35	100 50K IMO/50 EZ swim		7	2:00		5	2:15
		8	1:00		8	1:05	75 2x{1:DPS 2:Build 3:EZ 4:BLAST}		8	1:20		8	1:30
	2300	5	4:30	2000	4	4:55	300 (75D/75S)	1700	3	6:00	1550	3	6:45
		4	0:40		4	0:45	50		4	0:55		1	1:00
		3	2:30		3	2:45	200 Desc		3	3:20		3	3:45
	2300	1	500	2150	1	450	8:00 Pull every 3rd 25 Scull	1750	1	350	1500	1	300
		9	1:30		8	1:40	100 IM		5	2:00		3	2:15
		9	1:20		9	1:25	100 Desc 3		9	1:45		9	2:00

Set Type	Set Dist (Gold)	Repeats (Gold)	Interval (Gold)	Set Dist (Silver)	Repeats (Silver)	Interval (Silver)	SET	Set Dist (Bronze)	Repeats (Bronze)	Interval (Bronze)	Set Dist (Novice)	Repeats (Novice)	Interval (Novice)
General	2400	2x {4	2:45	2100	2x {3	3:05	{200 Distance Per Stroke	1800	2x {2	3:40	1600	2x {2	4:10
		{1	5:30		{1	6:05	{400 Pull		{1	7:20		{1	8:15
		-	-		2	0:50	50 GOLF		4	1:00		-	-
	2400	8	1:25	2100	7	1:35	100 Long & Strong, Stretch & Roll	1800	6	1:55	1600	6	2:05
		4	2:45		3	3:10	200 Focus Kicking and Tech		4	3:40		3	4:10
		2	5:20		2	5:50	400 Focus Tech and long strokes		1	7:05		1	8:00
	2400	3	600	2150	3	550	8:00 first 25 of each 100, IM cycle (skip free)	1750	3	450	1600	3	400
		6	1:25		5	1:35	100 Build		4	1:55		4	2:10
	2500	1	5:10	2300	1	5:40	400 Cruise	2000	1	6:50	1700	1	7:45
		2	3:55		2	4:20	300 Cruise		2	5:10		2	6:00
		3	2:40		3	2:55	200 Cruise		3	3:30		2	4:00
		4	1:25		4	1:35	100 Build		4	1:55		3	2:05
		5	1:30		3	1:40	100 IM		-	-		-	-
	2500	10	1:20	2300	9	1:30	100 K/S/D/S x25	2000	8	1:45	1800	7	2:00
		5	2:20		5	2:35	200 Cruise		5	3:10		5	3:30
		20	0:30		16	0:30	25 o:Stroke e:Free		8	0:35		4	0:45
	2600	8	1:20	2300	8	1:30	100 w/ Zoomers or Fins	2000	8	1:45	1700	5	2:00
		6	3:45		5	4:05	300 o:Pull e:Swim (Paddles Recommended)		4	4:55		4	5:30

Set Type	SET	Gold Set Dist	Gold Repeats	Gold Interval	Silver Set Dist	Silver Repeats	Silver Interval	Bronze Set Dist	Bronze Repeats	Bronze Interval	Novice Set Dist	Novice Repeats	Novice Interval
General	{10 sec between swim…efforts moderate												
	{100 Kick		1			1			1			1	
	{200 Pull		1			1			1			1	
	{300 Swim	2800	1		2800	1		2100	1		2100	1	
	{400 Pull w/ Paddles		1			1			1			1	
	{500 Swim w/ Paddles		1			1			1			1	
	{600 Swim w/ Fins		1			1			1			1	
	{700 Swim w/ Fins & Paddles		1			1			-			-	
Middle Distance	50 2:@30 (33,40,45) 1:@35 (39, 45,53)		9	0:45		9	0:50		9	0:55		9	1:05
	600 Pull (N=350)		1	8:25		1	9:15		1	10:40		1	7:30
	50 2:@30 (33,40,45) 1:@35 (39, 45,53)	2100	6	0:40	1900	6	0:45	1700	6	0:50	1450	6	1:00
	400 IM done as 100IM's (B&N=200)		1	6:30		1	7:10		1	4:30		1	5:00
	50 2:@30 (33,40,45) 1:@35 (39, 45,53)		3	0:35		3	0:40		3	0:45		3	0:55
	200 75S/25Bk		1	2:40		-	-		-	-		-	-
	{150 Descend		3x {4	2:00		3x {3	2:20		3x {3	2:45		3x {3	3:05
	{50 Build	2250	{3	0:55	1950	{4	0:55	1650	{2	1:10	1500	{1	1:15
	{Rest		{-	-		{R	0:05		{R	0:10		{R	0:15
	75 Cruise		6	1:05		6	1:10		4	1:25		4	1:40
	300 Descend	2250	2	4:05	2000	2	4:30	1650	2	5:25	1450	2	6:10
	50 o:Fly or Br e:Bk		6	0:50		5	0:55		5	1:05		3	1:15
	100 2,3,6-BLAST 9:Not Free		9	1:20		7	1:30		5	1:45		4	2:00
	50 Race Pace		9	0:45		10	0:50		8	1:00		8	1:05
	400 100's alt Kick/Swim (N=300)	2350	1	6:30	2100	1	7:00	1700	1	8:40	1600	1	7:20
	300 Moderate		5	3:45		4	4:05		3	5:00		3	5:40

Set Type		Gold			Silver		SET		Bronze			Novice	
	Set Dist	Repeats	Interval	Set Dist	Repeats	Interval		Set Dist	Repeats	Interval	Set Dist	Repeats	Interval
Middle Distance	2400	5	0:45	2100	4	0:50	50 cruise	1750	3	1:00	1550	3	1:10
		3	3:10		2	3:30	250 cruise		2	4:10		2	4:45
		4	1:25		4	1:35	100 IM		3	1:50		2	2:10
		3	1:40		3	1:50	150 25EZ/100Build/25Sprint		2	2:15		2	2:30
		4	0:50		4	0:55	50 Bk		3	1:05		2	1:15
		3	0:40		3	0:45	50 sub30 (33, 40, 45)		3	0:55		2	1:00
		4	0:30		4	0:35	25 IM Kick		4	0:40		4	0:45
		4	0:40		4	0:45	25 Sprint		4	0:55		4	1:00
	2450	1	5:00	2150	1	5:30	400 50EZ/25SP	1850	1	6:40	1600	1	7:30
		6	0:50		5	0:55	50 D/B		4	1:05		4	1:15
		7	3:10		6	3:30	250 100 strong, 100 build, 50 fast		5	4:10		4	4:45
	2450	4	1:20	2150	2	1:30	100's	1800	3	1:40	1650	3	2:00
		3	1:15		2	1:25	100's		2	1:35		2	1:55
		2	1:10		2	1:20	100's		1	1:25		1	1:45
		1	1:05		1	1:15	100's		-	-		-	-
		9	0:50		9	0:55	50 IM Rotation		6	1:05		3	1:15
		1	5:00		1	5:30	400 P		1	6:40		1	7:30
		1	3:45		1	4:10	300 S		1	5:00		1	5:40
		1	2:30		1	2:45	200 P		1	3:20		1	3:45
		1	1:15		1	1:25	100 S		-	-		-	-
Speed	1900	12	1:15	1700	12	1:20	75 Descend in sets of 3 {Strong, FAST, ALL OUT}	1400	12	1:40	1250	6	1:50
		4	1:45		4	1:55	100 Negative Split (50 cruise/50 BLAST)		3	2:20		4	2:35
		3	3:00		2	3:15	200 Monster Negative Split by 10+ sec		1	4:00		2	4:30
	2100	12	0:25	1800	12	0:30	25 Drills, every 4th DEAD SPRINT	1500	12	0:35	1300	12	0:35
		8	1:30		8	1:40	100 sub1:04 (1:10, 1:25, 1:36)		8	2:00		8	2:15
		2	5:20		1	5:50	400 Pull		1	7:05		-	-
		4	0:50		6	0:55	50 Dist Per Stroke		-	-		4	1:15

Set Type	SET	Gold Repeats	Gold Interval	Silver Repeats	Silver Interval	Bronze Repeats	Bronze Interval	Novice Repeats	Novice Interval
Speed	100 50FAST/50EZ	10	1:25	8	1:35	5	1:55	4	2:10
	200 EZ (N=150)	1	3:00	1	3:30	1	4:00	1	3:20
	75 ALL OUT	6	1:05	6	1:10	6	1:25	6	1:40
	200 EZ (N=150)	1	3:00	1	3:30	1	4:00	1	3:20
	100 Max Effort	4	1:12	3	1:18	3	1:35	3	1:50
	Set Dist	2250		1950		1650		1450	
	100 25 underwater ; r:05 ; 50BLAST ; 25EZ	8	1:30	8	1:40	7	2:00	6	2:20
	50 Drill	4	0:45	4	0:50	4	1:00	3	1:10
	100 25 underwater ; r:05 ; 50BLAST ; 25EZ	6	1:30	5	1:40	4	2:00	4	2:20
	150 100IM/50Free, LAST 25 ALL OUT	5	2:00	4	2:15	3	2:40	3	3:00
	Set Dist	2350		2100		1750		1600	
	250 200Build/50Sprint	4	3:15	4	3:35	3	4:20	3	4:55
	100 Kick BLAST (1-2&5-6 Free 3-4:Not Flutter)	6	1:50	6	2:05	5	2:25	4	2:45
	100 75Build/25Sprint	8	1:15	5	1:20	5	1:40	4	1:55
	Set Dist	2400		2100		1750		1550	
	75 (3 FAST, 1 EZ)	24	1:00	22	1:05	16	1:20	16	1:30
	200 #1:P #2:50K/50S (N=100)	2	3:15	2	3:35	2	4:20	2	2:30
	25 evens: BLAST odds:EZ	8	0:30	6	0:30	6	0:40	8	0:45
	Set Dist	2400		2200		1750		1650	
Short Rest Interval	100	7	1:15	5	1:25	4	1:40	4	1:55
	25 EZ	2	0:30	2	0:30	2	0:40	2	0:45
	100 Last 1 Fast	6	1:10	5	1:20	4	1:30	4	1:45
	50 25NotFree/25S	2	1:00	2	1:05	2	1:20	2	1:30
	100 Last 2 Fast	5	1:10	5	1:20	4	1:30	3	1:45
	25 EZ	2	0:30	2	0:30	2	0:40	2	0:45
	100 Last 3 Fast	4	1:15	5	1:25	4	1:40	3	1:55
	Set Dist	2400		2200		1800		1600	
		3x		3x		2x		2x	
	{250 Cruise	{2	3:15	{1	3:30	{2	4:15	{2	4:45
	{100 Strong	{2	1:10	{2	1:15	{2	1:30	{2	1:40
	{50 Blast	{2	0:33	{3	0:36	{2	0:43	{2	0:49
	{50 (S&B=100) Choice EZ	{1	1:14	{1	3:22	{1	3:44	{1	2:22
	Set Dist	2550		2100		1800		1700	

30-35 Minutes

Set Type	Gold Dist	Gold Repeats	Gold Interval	Silver Dist	Silver Repeats	Silver Interval	SET	Bronze Dist	Bronze Repeats	Bronze Interval	Novice Dist	Novice Repeats	Novice Interval
SRI	2800	5	2:50	2550	4	3:05	250 steady (but make the interval)	2000	4	4:05	1850	4	4:20
		5	1:55		5	2:05	150		4	2:45		3	2:50
		2	4:55		2	5:20	400 cruise hard		1	6:30		1	7:20
Stroke	1750	8	0:30	1600	6	0:30	25 o:Streamline Kick IM e:Drill IM	1400	6	0:40	1250	6	0:45
		2	0:25		2	0:30	25 EZ		2	0:35		2	0:35
		8	0:45		8	0:50	50 Switch IM (Fly/Bk, Bk/Br, Br/Fr, Fr/Fly..)		8	1:00		8	1:10
		2	0:35		2	0:35	25 Kick EZ (no board)		2	0:40		-	-
		8	1:10		6	1:15	50 Breast <or> Fly		2	1:30		-	-
		2	0:25		2	0:30	25 EZ		2	0:35		2	0:35
		8	1:20		8	1:30	75 Switch IM (Fly/Bk/Br, Bk/Br/Fr, Br/Fr/Fly..)		8	1:45		8	2:00
	2000	16	0:25	1750	10	0:25	25 Fly	1450	8	0:35	1300	8	0:40
		8	0:50		6	0:55	50 Breast		5	1:10		6	1:15
		4	1:30		4	1:40	100 IM		3	2:00		4	2:15
		2	3:15		2	3:40	200 Back		2	4:20		2	5:00
		1	6:15		1	7:00	400 IM (S=300)		1	6:15		-	-
	2000	8	1:40	1800	8	1:50	100 Back	1500	8	2:15	1400	8	2:30
		1	2:45		1	3:00	200 Free		1	3:40		1	4:10
		2	3:30		2	3:50	200 IM		2	4:40		2	5:15
		6	1:40		4	1:50	100 Breathe Every 5 or 7		1	2:20		-	-
	2000	1	5:00	1800	1	5:30	400 Free	1550	1	6:40	1400	1	7:30
		2	3:00		2	3:20	200 IM		2	4:00		2	4:30
		4	1:20		4	1:30	100 Free		3	1:45		3	2:00
		8	0:50		8	0:55	50 IM order		4	1:05		4	1:15
		16	0:30		8	0:35	25 Back		10	0:40		4	0:45

30-35 Minutes

Set Type	Gold Set Dist	Gold Repeats	Gold Interval	Silver Set Dist	Silver Repeats	Silver Interval	SET	Bronze Set Dist	Bronze Repeats	Bronze Interval	Novice Set Dist	Novice Repeats	Novice Interval
Stroke	2200	5	1:45	1900	4	1:55	100 Breaststroke last 1 fast	1600	3	2:20	1400	3	2:40
		10	0:55		8	1:00	50 Backstroke last 2 fast		6	1:15		5	1:25
		16	0:25		12	0:30	25 Fly last 4 fast		8	0:35		6	0:35
		8	1:25		8	1:35	100 IM's last 2 fast		8	1:55		7	2:10
	2200	2x		2000	2x		2x	1500	2x		1400	2x	
		{3	1:30		{4	1:40	{100 IM		{4	2:00		{3	2:15
		{3	3:00		{2	3:20	{200 IM		{1	4:00		{1	4:30
		{4	0:50		{4	0:55	{50 Back		{3	1:10		{4	1:20
	2250	6	2:00	2050	4	2:15	100 25K/50D/25S IM order	1650	4	2:40	1500	4	3:00
		1	5:00		1	5:30	400 Mod		1	6:40		1	7:30
		3	2:50		3	3:05	150 K build o:flutter e:dolphin <or> breast		3	3:50		2	4:25
		2	5:15		2	5:45	400 P BC3-5-3-7x50		1	7:00		1	7:55
	2300	7	4:20	2150	7	4:45	300 #1 - 25Fly/25Bk/25Br/225Fr {#2 - 50Fly/25Bk/25Br/200S {#3 - 75Fly/25Bk/25Br/175S {#4 - 75Fly/50Bk/25Br/150S {#5 - 75Fly/75Bk/25Br/125S {#6 - 75Fly/75Bk/50Br/100Fr, #7 - 300IM	1800	6	5:45	1550	5	6:30
	2400	4	0:55	2100	1	1:00	50 stroke SPRINT	1800	-	-	1500	1	1:30
	2400	3x		2100	3x		3x	1800	3x		1500	3x	
		{9	0:45		{7	0:50	{50 x(#1-Fly #2-Bk #3-Br)		{5	1:00		{6	1:15
		{1	5:00		{1	5:40	{300 Pull BC 5-3 x50 (N=200)		{1	6:30		{1	5:00
	2400	2x		2200	2x		2x	1800	2x		1600	2x	
		{1	5:40		{1	6:20	{400 IM		{1	7:40		-	-
		{2	2:50		{2	3:10	{200 IM		{1	3:50		{2	4:15
		{4	1:25		{3	1:35	{100 IM		{3	1:55		{4	2:10

		Gold			Silver			Bronze			Novice		
SET		**Rep**	**Dist**	**Int**	**Rep**	**Dist**	**Int**	**Rep**	**Dist**	**Int**	**Rep**	**Dist**	**Int**
6:10 Desc 1-4		4	500	1:15	4	450	1:20	4	375	1:40	4	325	2:00
50 Streamline Kick / Build w/ driving kick x25		10			9			7			6		
(Total)			2500			2250			1850			1600	
11:00 Steady (Long & Smooth Strokes)		1	800		1	750		1	600		1	550	
6:30 alt 50 BLAST/50 EZ		1	500		1	450		1	400		1	300	
100 FAST		3		1:30	3		1:40	3		2:00	2		2:15
50 cruise w/ 10 pushups, situps, & squats		5		1:30	5		1:35	5		1:45	4		2:15
150		1		2:10	1		2:20	1		2:40	1		3:05
150		1		2:05	1		2:15	1		2:35	1		2:55
150		1		2:00	1		2:10	1		2:30	1		2:45
150		1		1:55	1		2:05	-		-	-		-
150		1		1:50	-		-	-		-	-		-
(Total)			2600			2350			2000			1700	
9:30 Cruise		1	800		1	700		1	600		1	500	
50 o:EZ e:BLAST		10		0:45	7		0:50	6		1:00	6		1:10
100 Fast		3		1:30	3		1:40	3		2:00	3		2:10
300 descend (N=250)		4		4:00	4		4:25	3		5:20	3	250	5:00
(Total)			2800			2550			2100			1850	
100 Overkick		8		1:25	6		1:30	3		1:50	2		2:10
800 All out (N=600)		1		10:00	1		11:00	1		13:20	1	600	11:15
100 o:BK e: BR		4		1:45	4		1:55	3		2:20	3		2:45
800 Descend each 200		1		10:00	1		11:00	1		13:20	1		15:00
(Total)			2800			2600			2200			1900	
10:00 Steady		3	800		3	700		3	600		3	550	
Rest		R		0:30	-			R		0:30	-		
100 P		3		1:20	3		1:30	2		1:45	2		2:00
75 K		2		1:20	2		1:30	2		1:45	2		2:00
50 0 breaths down / 1 breath back (it is just 1)		1		0:45	1		0:50	-		-	-		-
(Total)			2900			2600			2150			2000	

Distance

35-40 Minutes

61

Set Type	SET	Gold Dist	Gold Repeats	Gold Interval	Silver Dist	Silver Repeats	Silver Interval	Bronze Dist	Bronze Repeats	Bronze Interval	Novice Dist	Novice Repeats	Novice Interval
Distance	800 Last 1 strong (N=650)		2	9:45		2	10:40		1	13:00		1	12:15
	250 Descend by 2sec each 50		4	3:15		3	3:35		4	4:20		4	5:00
	50 Bk		4	0:50		3	0:55		4	1:05		2	1:15
	25 Sprint	2900	4	0:40	2600	4	0:45	2100	4	1:00	1850	4	1:00
	100 25D/75S		4	1:30		3	1:40		-	-		-	-
	800 Moderate		1	10:25		1	11:30		1	13:45		1	15:30
	600 Build Moderate to Strong		1	7:50		1	8:30		1	10:20		1	11:50
	400 Strong		1	5:15		1	5:45		1	7:00		1	7:50
	200 last 100 FAST		1	3:10		1	3:30		1	4:10		1	4:45
	50 Descend last 5	2900	10	0:42	2650	7	0:45	2250	5	0:55	2000	-	-
	400 Negative Split & Descend		4	5:15		3	5:45		3	7:00		2	8:00
	300 250 strong, r:05, 50Sprint		3	3:55		3	4:20		3	5:10		3	6:00
	200 100Fr/100Bk		2	2:40		2	2:55		1	3:30		1	4:00
	100 IM	3000	1	1:20	2600	1	1:30	2300	-	-	2000	1	2:00
General	r:30 6x(100 BC3, alt 50 BC5,9)		1	1000		1	1000		1	500		-	-
	r:30 Xx(100 4 beat K, alt 50 6,8 beat K)		1	800		1	800		1	600		1	800
	r:30 6x(50 BC3, alt 50 BC5,7)		1	600		1	600		1	600		1	600
	r:30 4x(50 4 beat K, alt 50 6,8 beat K)		1	400		1	400		1	400		1	400
	r:30 BUST IT!	3000	1	200	3000	1	200	2300	1	200	2000	1	200
	100 IM		6	1:30		4	1:40		2	2:00		2	2:15
	250 #1-Pull #2-Paddles+Fins #3-Paddles+Fins {#4-Fins #5-Swim	2350	5	3:40	2050	5	4:00	1750	5	4:55	1650	5	5:30
	25 5 each stroke Descend each		20	0:30		16	0:35		12	0:40		8	0:45
	50 Kick o:dolphin on back e:Flutter on stomach		8	1:00		8	1:05		6	1:20		5	1:30
	200 Kick/IM order strong/Scull/Sprint Free}x50		7	3:00		6	3:20		5	4:00		5	4:30
	50 Drill		9	0:45		8	0:50		6	1:00		5	1:10
	25 SPRINT	2400	6	0:40	2150	6	0:45	1750	6	0:55	1600	4	1:00

Set Type	Gold Set Dist	Gold Repeats	Gold Interval	Silver Set Dist	Silver Repeats	Silver Interval	SET	Bronze Set Dist	Bronze Repeats	Bronze Interval	Novice Set Dist	Novice Repeats	Novice Interval
General	2500	4	2:45	2250	4	3:05	200 Pull 3rd 50 Fly	1850	3	3:40	1650	3	4:15
		1	600		1	550	8:00 strong (optional zoomers/fins/paddles)		1	450		1	400
		8	1:35		7	1:45	100 o:Stroke e:Free		6	2:10		4	2:20
		12	0:30		8	0:35	25 Kick w/ board		8	0:40		10	0:45
	2500	4	1:05	2350	4	1:10	75	1950	3	1:10	1700	3	1:35
		3	1:00		3	1:05	75		2	1:05		2	1:25
		2	0:55		2	1:00	75		1	1:00		1	1:15
		1	0:50		1	0:55	75		-	-		-	-
		4	1:50		4	2:00	125 Strong IM (50 of your race stroke)		4	2:25		2	2:45
		4	2:45		4	3:00	200 Negative Split & Descend		4	3:40		4	4:10
		6	0:55		3	1:00	50 Back		2	1:10		2	1:30
		6	0:40		6	0:40	25 BLAST		4	0:55		4	1:00
	2800	12	0:40	2500	10	0:45	50 Pace @ T30Pace (or mile+2s/50)	2100	8	0:55	1900	6	1:00
		10	1:20		8	1:30	100 Just Cruise		5	1:45		4	2:00
		4	4:00		4	4:25	300 #1-P #2-S #3-w/Fins #4-w/Fins&Paddles		4	5:20		4	6:00
	2850	2	3:55	2550	2	4:20	300 swim focus on kick	2100	2	5:15	1850	2	6:00
		1	7:30		1	8:15	600 each 100 SAME time (N=500)		1	10:00		1	10:00
		3	1:20		3	1:30	100 desc		3	1:45		3	2:00
		9	2:00		7	2:10	150 50S/25sprint/50S/25IM ROT		4	2:40		3	3:00
	2950	1	0:45	2750	1	0:50	50 10 strokes max per length	2250	3	0:55	2000	1	1:10
		2	2:05		3	2:15	150 Build		2	2:40		1	3:10
		3	3:25		3	3:40	250 Desc		3	4:25		3	4:40
		4	4:45		3	5:05	350 Desc		3	6:10		3	7:10
		1	5:30		1	6:05	450 cruise		-	-		-	-

Set Type	Gold Dist	Gold Repeats	Gold Interval	Silver Dist	Silver Repeats	Silver Interval	SET	Bronze Dist	Bronze Repeats	Bronze Interval	Novice Dist	Novice Repeats	Novice Interval
General	3050	9	2:30	2850	9	2:45	200 3x(1,2-Pull w/Paddles 3:Swim w/Paddles)	2200	6	3:20	2050	6	3:45
		6	1:25		4	1:35	75 K		4	1:55		2	2:00
		4	1:40		4	1:50	125 3rd:25IM		4	2:15		4	2:30
		6	0:40		5	0:45	50 SPRINT		4	1:00		4	1:00
	3300	3x		3100	2x		3x	2350	2x		1900	2x	
		{2	4:45		{2	5:15	{400 Pull w/ Paddles		{1	6:20		{1	7:10
		{2	2:35		{2	2:50	{200 Swim w/ Paddles		{2	3:30		{2	3:55
		{5	1:00		{3	1:05	{50 Kick (25 steady/25 build)		{4	1:20		{3	1:30
Middle Distance	2750	5	1:30	2500	5	1:35	100	2050	3	2:00	1900	3	2:15
		4	2:05		4	2:15	150		4	2:45		3	3:05
		5	3:10		4	3:25	250		3	4:10		3	4:45
		1	5:00		1	5:50	400		1	6:40		1	7:00
	2950	4	1:20	2700	3	1:30	100 Desc (N=Build)	2300	2	1:50	2050	1	2:00
		3	1:15		3	1:20	75 IM (G&S=no free, B&N=no fly)		2	1:40		2	1:50
		3	2:30		3	2:45	200 Desc		3	3:20		3	3:45
		3	1:15		3	1:20	75 IM		2	1:40		2	1:50
		3	500		3	450	6:20 Desc		3	400		3	350
Speed	2200	20	0:40	2000	20	0:40	25's from a dive	1500	20	0:55	1250	20	1:00
		8	1:50		8	2:00	125 25EZ/50build/25EZ/25BLAST		6	2:25		4	2:45
		2	4:30		2	3:45	350 (S,B,N=250) BC 5-3 x50		1	4:30		1	5:30
	2650	11	0:55	2500	8	1:00	50 Strong, last 4 BLAST broken @ 25 for 5 sec	2000	8	1:10	1600	8	1:30
		24	0:25		24	0:25	25 Swim - Kicking 1/2 way under water		24	0:30		16	0:40
		3	5:50		3	6:20	500 Swim (Optional Paddles) (N=400)		2	7:50		2	7:00

Set Type	SET	Gold Dist	Gold Repeats	Gold Interval	Silver Dist	Silver Repeats	Silver Interval	Bronze Dist	Bronze Repeats	Bronze Interval	Novice Dist	Novice Repeats	Novice Interval
Short Rest Intervals	50 ALL OUT	2700	10	1:05	2500	10	1:10	2050	8	1:25	1800	7	1:35
	75 EZ		8	1:05		8	1:10		6	1:25		6	1:35
	50 Strong		8	0:40		7	0:45		6	0:50		5	1:00
	100 Strong		8	1:15		7	1:20		6	1:35		5	1:50
	50 Strong		8	0:35		7	0:40		6	0:45		5	0:55
	200 o:build each 50 e:build by 50's	3000	5	2:35	2600	3	3:00	2200	3	3:30	2000	2	4:00
			5x			5x			4x			4x	
	{100 make it by 5 seconds		{2	1:12		{2	1:20		{2	1:35		{2	1:50
	{50 make it by 5 seconds		{2	0:37		{2	0:40		{2	0:48		{2	0:55
	{25 Sprint		{4	0:20		{4	0:22		{4	0:27		{4	0:30
	{Rest		{R	0:02		{R	0:02		{R	0:01		{R	-
Stroke	Rd1-Fly Rd2-Bk Rd3-Br	2300	3x		2150	3x		1800	3x		1500	3x	
	{25 Desc by 4's (last 2 All Out)		{10	0:30		{8	0:35		{6	0:40		{6	0:45
	{250 Perfect Stroke Cruise (N=150)		{1	4:00		{1	4:25		{1	5:20		{1	3:40
			2x			2x			2x			2x	
	{200 IM		{1	3:00		{1	3:20		{1	4:00		{1	4:30
	{100 IM Build each 25		{2	1:30		{2	1:40		{1	2:00		{1	2:15
	{Rd1:Fly Rd2:Bk Rd3:Br	2400	3x		2200	3x		1750	3x		1650	3x	
	{75 1-2:last 25 Sprint, Last 4:Descend		{8	1:15		{8	1:20		{6	1:40		{6	1:50
	{REST		{R	0:20		{R	0:20		{R	0:20		{R	0:20
	100 Choice EZ		1	2:00		1	2:10		1	2:40		-	-
	100 Swim w/ 2 Butterfly Kicks off each wall (Zoomers Optional)		5	1:20		3	1:25		3	1:45		3	2:00

Set Type	SET	Gold Set Dist	Gold Repeats	Gold Interval	Silver Set Dist	Silver Repeats	Silver Interval	Bronze Set Dist	Bronze Repeats	Bronze Interval	Novice Set Dist	Novice Repeats	Novice Interval
20x100 Series	100 Best Average	3100	20	1:25	2800	20	1:35	2350	16	1:55	2100	14	2:10
	25 IM order <or> Choice EZ		8	0:35		8	0:35		6	0:40		4	0:45
	300 Descend		3	3:50		2	4:15		2	5:15		2	5:45
	100 Best Average	3200	5	1:30	2950	5	1:35	2450	4	1:50	2150	4	2:10
	100 |		5	1:25		5	1:30		4	1:45		4	2:05
	100 |		5	1:20		5	1:25		4	1:40		3	2:00
	100 V		5	1:15		5	1:20		4	1:35		3	1:55
	25 IM order (kick the first 1/2 of each 25)		8	0:30		6	0:35		10	0:40		6	0:45
	200 1-3:Descend, The Rest are last 50 Sprint		5	2:40		4	2:55		3	3:40		3	4:00
	100 Goal:7+sec Rest	3250	5	1:30	2950	5	1:35	2550	3	1:45	2200	4	2:05
	100 | This is a failure set		4	1:25		4	1:30		3	1:40		3	2:00
	100 | your job is to succeed		3	1:20		3	1:25		3	1:35		2	1:55
	100 |		2	1:15		2	1:20		2	1:30		1	1:50
	100 V		1	1:10		1	1:15		1	1:25		-	–
	100 Make it Baby		5	1:05		5	1:10		4	1:20		4	1:45
	50 Choice EZ (at least 25 of each 50 Not Free)		7	1:00		7	1:05		7	1:20		4	1:30
	300 1-3: Descend with the 1st & Last 25 Sprint		3	3:50		2	4:15		2	5:15		2	5:45
	{100 Best Average	3350	5x {1	1:25	3100	5x {1	1:30	2550	4x {1	1:40	2200	3x {2	2:05
	{100 |		{1	1:20		{1	1:25		{1	1:35		{1	2:00
	{100 |		{1	1:15		{1	1:20		{1	1:30		{1	1:55
	{100 V		{1	1:10		{1	1:15		{1	1:25		{1	1:50
	75 50Choice/25K EZ		2	1:30		4	1:25		2	2:00		2	2:00
	400 Negative Split (N=325)		3	5:20		2	5:50		2	7:20		2	6:30

Set Type	Gold Set Dist	Gold Repeats	Gold Interval	Silver Set Dist	Silver Repeats	Silver Interval	SET	Bronze Set Dist	Bronze Repeats	Bronze Interval	Novice Set Dist	Novice Repeats	Novice Interval
20x100 Series	3250	4	1:30	3000	4	1:40	100 EZ	2300	-	-	2150	3	2:15
		1	1:05		1	1:10	100 Fast		1	1:25		1	1:45
		3	1:30		3	1:40	100 EZ		3	2:00		2	2:15
		2	1:05		2	1:10	100 Fast		2	1:25		2	1:45
		2	1:30		2	1:40	100 EZ		2	2:00		1	2:15
		3	1:05		3	1:10	100 Fast		3	1:25		3	1:45
		1	1:30		1	1:40	100 EZ		1	2:00		1	2:15
		4	1:05		4	1:10	100 Fast		4	1:25		1	1:45
		5	1:00		4	1:05	50 Backstroke / Streamline kick x25		2	1:20		3	1:30
		5	2:40		4	2:55	200 Desc 1-3 ; 4-5 last 100 Fast		3	3:40		3	4:00
Distance	3000	3	1000	2700	3	900	odds: Swim on 12:45, evens: IM on 15:00	2250	3	750	1950	3	650
		{4	100		{3	100	{EZ ALL IM's on round 2 done as 100 IM's		{3	100		{3	100
		{3	100		{3	100	{Strong		{2	100		{2	100
		{2	100		{2	100	{FAST		{2	100		{1	100
		{1	100		{1	100	{ALL OUT (B&N: round 2-Race Stroke)		{1	50		{1	50
	3300	1	1:05	3000	1	1:10	100	2500	1	1:30	2200	1	1:45
		2	1:10		1	1:15	100		2	1:35		2	1:50
		3	1:15		2	1:20	100		3	1:40		3	1:55
		4	1:20		3	1:25	100		-	-		1	2:00
		5	5:30		5	6:05	400 #1:400S #2:300S/100IM...#5:400IM		4	7:20		3	8:15
		4	1:05		4	1:10	75 Pull Fr/Bk/Fr DAS		4	1:25		4	1:40
	3400	4	3:45	3000	4	4:10	300 Strong	2550	3	5:00	2250	3	5:45
		8	1:00		8	1:05	75 FAST		6	1:20		2	1:30
		4	5:10		3	5:40	400 o:Swim e:Pull		3	6:50		3	7:45

Set Type	Gold Set Dist	Gold Repeats	Gold Interval	Silver Repeats	Silver Interval	SET	Bronze Repeats	Bronze Interval	Bronze Set Dist	Novice Repeats	Novice Interval	Novice Set Dist
		1	800	1	700	9:30 FAST	1	600		1	550	
		4	1:45	4	1:55	100 o:BK e:BR	3	2:20		3	2:45	
		1	800	1	700	10:30 desc by 200	1	600		1	550	
		10	0:45	10	0:50	50 o:Sprint e:EZ	10	1:00		10	1:15	
		4	3:00	3	3:15	200 Medley Relay order (Bk/Br/Fly/Fr)	2	4:00		1	5:00	
	3400	1	1:30	1	1:40	100 ALL OUT	1	2:00	2500	1	2:15	2200
		1	6:40	1	7:30	500 BC3-5-3-7x50	1	8:45		1	10:00	
		2	5:20	2	6:00	400 Pull Building each 100	1	7:00		1	8:00	
		3	4:00	3	4:30	300 25EZ/50Sprint	2	5:15		2	6:00	
		4	2:40	4	3:00	200 1,2:w/paddles 3,4:No paddles ; O:S E:Pull	3	3:30		3	4:00	
		R	0:20	R	0:30	REST	R	0:30		R	0:30	
	3500	5	1:20	1	1:30	100 @T30 Pace	5	1:45	2600	2	2:00	2300
		12	0:30	10	0:35	25 breakout past flags, kick from flags to wall	8	0:40		8	0:45	
	3500	4	800	4	725	11:00 Every 4th 25 = #1-Fly #2-Bk #3-Br #4-Bk	4	600	2600	4	550	2400
		4	4:45	3	5:15	400 Cruise	2	6:20		2	7:10	
		1	3:15	1	3:35	200 IM EZ	1	4:20		1	5:00	
		3	3:35	3	3:55	300 Cruise	2	4:50		2	4:55	
		1	3:10	1	3:30	200 IM EZ	1	4:10		1	5:00	
		2	2:25	2	2:40	200 Cruise	2	3:10		2	3:40	
		1	3:05	1	3:25	200 IM EZ	1	4:00		1	5:00	
		1	1:15	1	1:25	100 Cruise	2	1:40		1	1:55	
	3800	1	3:00	1	3:20	200 IM BLAST	1	3:50	2800	-	-	2500
		10	1:20	10	1:30	100 sub1:08 (1:15, 1:31, 1:42)	4	1:45		5	2:00	
		4	4:50	3	5:20	400 @4:45 (5:13, 6:20, 7:08)	3	6:25		2	7:15	
		4	1:00	4	1:05	75 @45 (50, 1:00, 1:08)	4	1:20		4	1:30	
	3900	2	6:30	2	7:10	500 Pull	2	8:40	2900	2	9:45	2600

Set Type	SET	Gold Dist/Rep	Gold Int	Silver Dist/Rep	Silver Int	Bronze Dist/Rep	Bronze Int	Novice Dist/Rep	Novice Int
		4 1000		4 900		4 700		4 650	
Distance	12:15 #1:Continuous #2:broken500r:15 #3:broken200r:10 #4:broken100r:05	4000		3600		2800		2600	
	100 IM	4	1:20	4	1:25	4	1:45	3	2:00
	200 100IM/100Fr	3	2:35	3	2:45	3	3:25	2	4:00
	300 100IM/200Fr	2	3:50	2	4:05	2	5:05	1	6:00
	400 100IM/300Fr	1	5:05	1	5:25	1	6:45	-	-
	400 Strong	1	5:00	-	-	-	-	1	7:40
	300 FAST	2	3:45	2	4:00	1	5:00	2	5:45
	200 FAST	3	2:30	3	2:40	2	3:20	2	3:50
	100 FAST	4	1:15	5	1:20	3	1:40	2	1:55
		4000		3700		2800		2500	
	50's are EZ, desc each interval, 600's are MAX	3x		3x		2x		3x	
	{50	{1	0:40	{2	0:45	{2	0:55	{3	1:00
	{100	{1	1:20	{1	1:25	{2	1:45	{1	2:00
	{200	{1	2:25	{-	-	{1	3:15	{1	3:40
	{400	{1	4:50	{1	5:20	{1	6:25	{1	7:15
	{600	{1	7:10	{1	8:00	{1	9:35	{-	-
	{Rest for a few breaths	{R	0:15	{R	0:25	{R	0:25	{R	0:25
		4050		3600		3000		2550	

Set Type	Gold Dist	Gold Repeats	Gold Interval	Silver Dist	Silver Repeats	Silver Interval	SET	Bronze Dist	Bronze Repeats	Bronze Interval	Novice Dist	Novice Repeats	Novice Interval
General		8	0:40		6	0:45	50 Cruise		4	1:00		5	1:00
		-	-		-	-	25 Bk Pull w/ Paddles		1	0:35		1	0:35
		3	500		3	450	6:15 Pull w/ Paddles		3	375		3	325
	2800	3	0:55	2500	3	1:00	50 Bk	2150	3	1:15	1850	2	1:15
		1	8:00		1	8:50	450 Kick Pyramid (Fins optional) (N=300)		1	10:40		1	8:00
		3	0:55		3	1:00	50 Bk		3	1:15		2	1:15
		6	0:40		4	0:45	25 BLAST		2	1:00		4	1:00
		3	5:20		3	5:55	400 BC 3/5/7/9 x25 w/ Paddles		2	7:10		2	8:00
	3000	3	4:00	2700	3	4:25	300 Pull w/ Paddles	2300	3	5:20	2000	2	6:00
		3	3:15		2	3:35	200 Kick/Swim x50's (Fins Optional)		2	4:20		2	4:50
		3	2:00		2	2:15	100 w/Fins (25 Underwater, 25 Swim)		2	2:30		2	3:00
	3000	10	1:35	2700	7	1:45	100 25K/50D/25B	2300	7	2:05	2000	4	2:20
		5	5:35		5	6:10	400 (100 reverse IM, 200 Neg Split, 100 IM)		4	7:30		4	8:30
		2x			2x				2x			1x	
	3100	{2	3:30	2850	{2	3:50	{250 150 Build by 50, 50 Blast, 50 EZ	2350	{1	4:40	2100	{3	5:15
		{1	3:45		{1	4:05	{300 Race Pace w/zoomers or Fins or Paddles		{1	5:00		{2	5:40
		{6	1:50		{5	2:00	{125 75 Build by 25, 25 Blast, 25 EZ		{5	2:25		{6	2:45
		10	1:40		9	1:50	100 25K/50B/25Sprint		4	2:10		2	2:25
		2x			2x		EZ Cruise		2x			2x	
	3400	{1	5:10	3100	{1	5:40	{400	2600	{1	6:50	2400	{1	7:45
		{2	2:35		{2	2:50	{200		{2	3:45		{2	3:55
		{4	1:20		{3	1:25	{100		{3	1:45		{3	2:00
Mild Dist		4	3:50		3	4:10	300 Descend		3	5:05		3	5:45
	3400	8	1:00	3100	8	1:05	75 FAST using good form	2550	6	1:20	2300	8	1:30
		4	5:00		4	5:30	400 Swim (w/ Paddles if desired)		3	6:20		2	7:30

Type	Gold Set Dist	Gold Repeats	Gold Interval	Silver Set Dist	Silver Repeats	Silver Interval	SET	Bronze Set Dist	Bronze Repeats	Bronze Interval	Novice Set Dist	Novice Repeats	Novice Interval
Mid Dist	3500	12	1:20	3150	11	1:30	100 with FINS, DPS	2700	9	1:45	2400	6	2:00
		1	1:10		1	1:15	50 Bk EZ		1	1:35		1	1:45
		2	7:20		2	8:00	600 DPS w/ Paddles		2	9:45		2	11:00
		1	1:10		1	1:15	50 Bk EZ		1	1:35		1	1:45
		8	1:40		6	1:50	125 with FINS- 3rd 25- fly		4	2:15		4	2:30
Short Rest Interval	4000	4	0:35	3600	4	0:38	50 Desc	3000	4	0:45	2650	4	0:55
		3	2:30		2	2:45	200 Desc		2	3:20		2	3:45
		2	5:10		2	5:40	400 Neg Split		2	6:50		2	7:45
		1	10:50		1	11:50	800 EZ (N=600)		1	14:20		1	12:15
		2	5:05		2	5:35	400 Faster than 1st 400		1	6:40		1	7:40
		3	2:25		2	2:40	200 Fastest yet		1	3:10		1	3:40
		4	0:32		4	0:35	50 Pour it on		4	0:40		1	0:50
Stroke	2700	3x		2400	3x		Rd1-Fly Rd2-Bk Rd3-Br	1950	3x		1800	3x	
		{8	0:45		{6	0:50	{50 Desc 1-4, 5-X		{8	1:00		{7	1:10
		{4	2:00		{4	2:15	{125 IM (50 of strong stroke)		{2	2:40		{2	2:55
	2800	8	1:25	2450	7	1:35	100 50 Stroke/50 Free (stroke is fast)	2050	6	1:50	1850	5	2:10
		8	1:20		7	1:30	100 25 Stroke/75 Free (stroke is fast)		6	1:45		5	2:00
		6	1:10		5	1:20	100 All Free		4	1:35		4	1:50
		8	1:20		7	1:30	75 Kick		6	1:45		6	2:00
		-	-		1	0:20	25 Choice		-	-		-	-

71

40-50 Minutes

Glossary

G = Gold   **S = Silver**   **B = Bronze**   **N = Novice**

Ascend	- Each repeat gets slower
@##	- Paced swim at a specified time
BK	- Backstroke
Blast	- Maximal effort, not worried about form
BR	- Breaststroke
Breath Control	- (BC) Number of strokes between breaths
Build (B)	- A steadily increasing effort over the each repeat, start easy and build to a sprint
Catchup	- Swim one arm at a time tapping the other hand at entry initiating next stroke
Choice	- Any stroke including freestyle
Cruise	- An effort that is speedy but not fatiguing
Desc	- Descend, each repeat gets faster than previous
Dolphin kick	- Butterfly kick, a wave like motion from your hips
Double Turn	- Repeats that starts from either the flags or mid pool used to work on turns
DPS	- Distance per stroke, minimize strokes per length
EZ	- Effortless swim while keeping form
Fast	- Hard effort focused on maintaining maximum speed without losing form
Flutter Kick	- Freestyle kick, a scissor type kick coming from your hips
Golf	- Add up the number of strokes and your time, try to minimize your score
Heads Up	- Swim done with the chin out, head held steady out of the water, commonly known as sighting
Hold	- Maintain a certain pace
IM	- Individual Medley, lengths of Fly, Back, Breast, Free in that order (100 = 25 each, 200 = 50 each)
IM order	- One repeat of each Fly, Back, Breast, Free in order
IM rotation	- Repeats split into Fly/Bk, Bk/Br, Br/Fr, Fr/Fly

Kick (K)	- Isolation of the legs usually done with your back or with a board
Loosen	- Variable paced swim preparing for a maximal effort swim
Moderate	- An effort that can be maintained for a long period of time
MR order	- Repeats done as Back, Breast, Fly, Free
Neg Sp	- Negative Split, second half of the repeat is measurably faster than the first half
Overkick	- Swim with increased kick frequency and force
Perfect Stroke	- Increased focus on perfection of technique
Pull (P)	- Isolation of arms using a buoy to float the legs with the absence of kick
r:##	- Rest interval for ## seconds
Recovery	- An effort somewhere between swim and float
Reverse IM	- Done as Free, Breast, Back, Fly
Sprint	- Maximal effort while maintaining form
Steady	- A sustainable effort
Streamline	- Arms above head with elbows squeezing ears
Stroke	- Not freestyle
Strong	- A controlled hard effort, 80% of maximum effort
Strong IM	- Do additional lengths of strongest stroke(s) (ie 50Fly/25Bk/25Br/25Fr)
Strong Stroke	- Race stroke, not free
sub##	- Swim faster than ##
Swim (S)	- Normal Freestyle without equipment
T##	- A timed swim for ## minutes with the goal to cover maximal distance
Tarzan	- Swim with chin on the surface of the water with an accelerated kick
Tech	- Technique, usually drilling the weakest part of stroke
Timed	- All out benchmarks against the clock
Under/Over	- First half of the REPEAT underwater, finish with a strong swimming effort

Made in the USA
Lexington, KY
14 December 2012